INSIDE VICTORIA

Also by Bob Bottom

Behind the Barrier
The Godfather in Australia
Without Fear or Favour
Connections
Connections II
Shadow of Shame
Bugged

Edited:
Big Shots (David Wilson and Lindsay Murdoch)
Big Shots II (David Wilson and Paul Robinson)

Also by Tom Noble

Untold Violence

INSIDE VICTORIA

A CHRONICLE OF SCANDAL

BOB BOTTOM

with

JOHN SILVESTER

TOM NOBLE & PAUL DALEY

Pan

B&M

First published in 1991 by Pan Macmillan Publishers Australia
a division of Pan Macmillan (Australia) Pty Limited
6371 Balfour Street, Chippendale NSW 2008
in association with
Books & Magazines Pty Ltd
PO Box 337, Seaford, Victoria 3198

National Library of Australia cataloguing-in-publication data

Inside Victoria : a chronicle of scandal.
Includes index.
ISBN 0 330 27261 6
1. Corruption (in politics) – Victoria – History. 2. Organised crime – Victoria – History. 3. Police corruption – Victoria – History. 4. Victoria – Politics and government. I. Bottom, Bob.
364.1

Typeset in New Century Schoolbook and **Franklin Gothic**.
Edited, designed, composed and typeset by Pagemasters, Melbourne.
Linotronic output by OnTheBall, Melbourne.
Printed in Australia by The Book Printer, Maryborough.
Cover artwork by Bruce Davidson.

Contents

Credits

In the compilation of *Inside Victoria*, Bob Bottom wrote seven chapters – 1: Legacy of Victorianism, 2: The Bolte Era, 3: The Hamer Days, 4: The Cain Ascendancy, 9: Illegal Privilege, 19: Shadow over Opposition, and 19: State of Despair.
John Silvester wrote six chapters – 5: Stinky Limits, 7: Illegal Gambling, 10: Lord Mayoral Embarrassment, 11: Nunawading Affair, 12: Continental Scandal, and 16: The VEDC Debacle.
Tom Noble wrote four chapters – 6: Legalised Vice, 7: Illegal Drugs, 15: WorkCare Blow-out, and 17: Loss of State Bank.
Paul Daley wrote three chapters – 13: Departure of a Governor, 14: The NSCA Disaster, and 18: Pyramid Collapse.

1
Legacy of Victorianism

Although geographically at the bottom of Australia, Victoria has always tended to look down on other States, with its capital, Melbourne, perpetuating an aura of true Victorianism. In his book *Land of Fortune*, British journalist Jonathan Aitken wrote: 'If Queen Victoria were still alive, not only would she approve of Melbourne, she would probably feel more at home there than in any other city of her former Empire.'

American evangelist Billy Graham lauded it as 'one of the most moral cities I have seen'.

Just as the puritanical facade of the British Empire's Victorian Age belied festering vice and corruption behind the scenes, Australia's Victoria likewise has always had its hidden side.

Notwithstanding the fact that Victoria has always looked askance at New South Wales and other States because of their convict foundations, Victoria itself was founded upon illegality.

John Batman, who has been credited with being the founder of the settlement of Port Phillip, actually was a trespasser from Tasmania who claimed ownership in 1835 on behalf of private interests in already settled Tasmania. Funded by the Port Phillip Association of Van Diemen's Land, Batman conned uneducated Aborigines into signing away 600,000 acres of prime land in return for 100 pounds of flour, six shirts, 200 handkerchiefs, 20 pairs of blankets, 50 pairs of scissors, 30 mirrors, 30 tomahawks and 100 knives.

It was a deal the ruling colonial administration in Sydney proclaimed 'null and void', but it did not stop an invasion of pastoralists and their sheep from Tasmania, and within 15 years Victoria was officially declared a British colony in its own right, freeing Victoria from rule from Sydney and annexation as another convict settlement. With the discovery of gold a year later, Victoria's population shot up to nearly half that for the whole of Australia in less than a decade.

Melbourne became the bigger city of the continent, flaunting its pride by staging an international exhibition of 32,000 exhibits in its own new Exhibition Building. One exhibit that remains as a symbol of the age is a painting of a nude woman, Chloe, still hanging in Young and Jackson's pub on the corner of Swanson and Flinders Streets.

Not surprisingly, that era spawned a litany of scandals.

One inquiry investigated colonial politicians over allegations that the symbol of early democracy, the parliamentary mace, had been mislaid in Madame Brussell's brothel, one of a row of brothels within sight of Parliament House. Political suspects were absolved, but the mace never was recovered.

Visiting evangelist Henry Varley, who obviously saw more than Billy Graham was to see later, was quoted as saying he knew of no other city the size of Melbourne that had so many prostitutes.

When economic recession loomed throughout Australia in the 1890s, Victoria fell hardest, having spawned giddy real estate and company speculation in a cycle not unlike that to be repeated 100 years later.

In the fallout of the colonial episode, banks were bankrupted, and politicians, some of them directly responsible, resigned to escape retribution.

Melbourne's financial woes so tarnished its reputation

that it became a catchcry in debate that prolonged moves towards Federation. In November 1893, the *Bulletin* claimed that Federation was at that time unthinkable because Victoria would 'taint the continent with Victoria's foulness' and would mean 'taking over the bulk of Victoria's stink'. The *Bulletin* suggested: 'Victoria should be declared an infected province until its moral character has been renovated and its reputation restored ...'

When Federation was achieved in 1901, Victoria had recovered to be granted status as temporary capital of the new independent Australia. It was to last for 27 years, until the setting aside of the Australian Capital Territory within NSW and the building of the first Commonwealth Parliament in Canberra.

Over the years, everything that has gone on in other States also has occurred in Victoria, except that, traditionally, anything has been tolerated in Victoria only so long as it has been kept in place.

In truth, Victoria remains something of a class society.

According to Jonathan Aitken, 'what keeps Melbourne in its outwardly frozen state of puritanical conservatism is the holier-than-thou alliance of the suburban squares and the society snobs'. It is an enduring truism. While the neighbouring State of NSW and its much exposed capital, Sydney, has long exhibited a classless, if not brash society, Melbourne clings to its class distinctions, exemplified by its snobbish clubs.

Such an environment has nurtured a curious reluctance to muddy the waters in its own backyard.

In contrast to gregarious Sydney, where endemic police corruption has been recognised since the pattern established upon early settlement by the corrupt Rum Corp, the lingering class consciousness of Melbourne has tended to shelter a more distinct police class, accentuating the protective brotherhood syndrome of any police force, and thus mask more subtle, less penetrable cells of corrupt influences.

If police corruption in particular can reflect the state of society, as has been the perennial barometer for assessing the state of NSW, Victoria has never been immune from its sinister implications. Nor has Victoria been free of a strange degree of tolerance of criminality.

It was in Victoria that the term 'larrikin' was coined, by an Irish cop named Dalton from Kilkenny in Ireland, as a description of Irish criminals who liked to portray themselves as rebels fighting for justice.

Throughout the 1800s, various public inquiries were conducted into Victorian police activities, establishing that corrupt practices emerged virtually from the outset of Victoria's settlement. For a crucial 22 years until 1880, the force had one continuous Chief Commissioner, Frederick Standish. As observed in Robert Haldane's authoritative and independent history of the force in his book *The People's Force*, the reign of Standish 'lulled many people into thinking that all was as well as possible with the colony's police, quite a few of whom had been basking comfortably in a widespread belief that Victoria's police were the finest in Australia'.

It was only through inquiries following his resignation in 1880 that action was taken to eliminate corrupt elements and improve the force.

It was the historic episode involving bushranger Ned Kelly that provided a catalyst for a clean-up of the force.

Son of an Irish convict, Kelly, and his gang, confronted the police and engaged in robbery and murder. In an ultimate showdown, three of his outlaw gang – Dan Kelly, Steve Hart and Joe Byrne – died in a police siege at Glenrowan on 26 June 1880. Wounded, Kelly was hanged for murder at Melbourne jail on 11 November 1880.

In the meantime, within weeks of Glenrowan, Standish was forced to retire, with agitation forcing a Royal Commission into events surrounding the Kelly affair. The commission sat for two years, leading also to the retirement of two superintendents and other officers, and a reorganisation of the force.

The commission categorised Ned Kelly as having 'led a wild and reckless life, and was always associated with the dangerous characters' and it concluded that the Kelly gang episode derived from police actions that 'weakened that effective and complete surveillance without which the criminal classes in all countries become more and more restive and defiant of the authorities'. At the same time, the commission served a purpose in focusing on police corruption. It brought about disgrace of one superintendent, Fred Winch, who had a history of corrupt behaviour extending over 20 years. Winch accepted bribes to allow sly grogging, prostitution and illegal gambling to flourish in Melbourne, and he was found to have interfered with honest police doing their job 'to grapple with the evil'. On one occasion, Winch was discovered by a young constable inside a brothel, actually in a private room guarded by Madame Brussell.

As was to happen all too often in Victoria and elsewhere in subsequent times, Winch was allowed to retire with a pension, without charges.

In their book *The Bushrangers*, William Joy and Tom Prior wrote: 'Most Australians remember Ned Kelly as an Australian, not as the son of an Irish convict; as a superb bushman, not as a "flash larrikin"; and as a brave man who was loyal to his family and friends, not as a thief and murderer.' More pointedly, Henry Giles Turner in *A History of the Colony of Victoria* wrote that the Kelly episode 'revealed one regrettable trait in the character of a Victorian crowd, an ingrained sympathy with defiance of the law ...' Turner pondered: 'The fact that the territory that bred them held scores of active and avowed sympathisers with their lawless career gave cause for anxious reflection as to how deep the taint of imported convictism might have penetrated ... the outlaws had so many sympathisers throughout the country that every movement of the police was anticipated and every action frustrated'.

The Kelly gang operations represented probably the first real manifestation of community tolerance or protection of organised criminals as such in Australia. The hanging of Kelly brought an end to the bushranger era in Victoria.

In his wake emerged a more enduring identity, John Wren, who eschewed confrontation in favour of corruption to exploit the larrikin underbelly of Victoria to forge a formidable empire, including the conduct of a large-scale illegal totalisator at Collingwood that was uninterrupted for nearly 15 years. A Royal Commission in 1905 investigated the inability of police to close Wren's tote, but Wren was not even called to give evidence.

The commission found that police were left powerless to suppress Wren's activities because of inefficiency of legislation, meaning that Wren enjoyed protection not so much from police but from politicians.

A public furore finally forced Parliament to enact a Lotteries Gaming and Betting Act, which enabled police to close down Wren's tote in 1907. About 70 police with battering rams and guns raided the tote. 'Not since the Kelly days had the police been forced to combine, plan and operate on such a scale,' wrote Haldane in *The People's Force*.

According to Haldane, it ended 'a unique phase in the development of policing in Victoria and signalled the dawn of a new era. Policemen had been confronted by organised criminals who treated illegal activity as commercial enterprise and used the combined skills of lawyers, politicians, petty gangsters and corrupt officials. Wren's team flagrantly exploited and flouted inadequate legislation to make illegal gambling a profitable business, doing so on a scale that individual policemen could scarcely comprehend, let alone counter. Wren's operations fit the classic organised crime mould common in the 1980s but, until the time of Wren, policemen had principally dealt with crime and criminals on an individual level ...'.

In 1950, when Frank Hardy published his famous novel *Power Without Glory*, a fictionalised version of Wren's power, Hardy was vilified in Parliament by politicians of all parties. Prosecuted for criminal libel, he was acquitted by a jury in June 1951. In a letter to the *Argus*, a former Liberal member of parliament, John Lechte, wrote: 'The continued attempts to suppress the publication of the book *Power Without Glory*, along with the implication made under protection of parliamentary privilege that the jury were wrong in their verdict at the trial of Frank Hardy, will surely give food for thought to all freedom-loving people ... That he hit where it hurts most in his description of the political scene, especially in Victoria, is apparent ... Anyone who has the briefest experience, however, of public affairs and political life trusts that more works will flow from the pen of this brave man and that this may be the beginning of a clean-up of our political cesspool and the farcical party system of Government that operates to deny the wishes of the people.'

A political casualty of the early part of the Wren era was Sir Samuel Gillott, who, as Chief Secretary of Victoria, had charge of passage of the bill designed to suppress Wren's tote. His administration had been singled out for criticism. Amid the plethora of allegations, Gillott resigned after being exposed as having financial dealings with Melbourne's most notorious brothel operator, Madame Brussell. Not only did he look after her as a client through his legal practice, but also he was mortgagee of her brothel premises. Gillott served three terms as Lord Mayor of Melbourne. The legal firm he founded continued under his name until the 1980s, attracting prestigious clients.

Historical records indicate that elements within the police themselves subsequently became more organised, and not necessarily for good purposes. Scrutiny of corrupt elements within the force provoked a strike by hundreds of police in 1923 – the first and only police strike in Australian history. More than 600 police struck in protest against the appointment of senior constables, denounced by entrenched police as 'special supervisors' or 'spooks'.

Unrest over police conditions was exploited by police elements protecting brothels and illegal gambling establishments.

Four senior constables were appointed to work in plain clothes with a roving commission to supervise police on the beat, amid complaints of police 'idling about the streets, leaning against lamp posts' and 'drunk at night'. One constable had been caught committing a warehouse robbery, in daylight, in his uniform.

In Parliament, in the same way as politicians used to defend John Wren, the police supervisors were opposed as 'pimps'. Nonetheless, in a purge of licensing police, 17 officers were transferred. When 636 police refused to go on duty unless the supervisors were removed, they were sacked, never to be allowed back into the force.

During the strike, crowds went berserk. Two men were killed and shops plundered in an orgy of looting. Throughout the first six days of November 1923, Lieutenant Sir John Monash was authorised to swear in 5000 officers from his soldier days as a Special Constabulary Force to quell the lawlessness.

After a Royal Commission, which recommended changes,

a succession of outsiders were to be put in charge of the force for the next half century.

Yet the system of supervisors was abandoned, never to be reintroduced, which probably helps to explain the rise to power of Squizzy Taylor, glorified by some Victorians as a sort of folk hero like Ned Kelly.

Born eight years after the hanging of Kelly, Taylor gained his initiation into crime as a teenager through turn-of-the-century gangs, as a member of the 'Bourke Street Rats', who preyed on people along Bourke Street in proximity to police-protected brothels, gambling houses and Chinese opium dens.

In time, he graduated from pick-pocketing, petty theft and standover activities to murder, assaults, armed robbery, arson, blackmail, witness bashing, bribery, perjury, jury rigging, race fixing, illegal gambling, prostitution and drug dealing – and he was a police informer to boot.

As gangland leader, Taylor provided muscle for a network of illegal enterprises in partnership with Henry Stokes, who had succeeded John Wren as the city's czar of illegal gambling.

An attempt by Melbourne trendies to feature Taylor in a film in 1922 prompted the then Victorian Chief Secretary, Major M. Baird, to intervene to stop its production.

Cooperating with journalists who favoured him, a pattern adopted by latter-day crime bosses in Sydney, Taylor was to proclaim: 'I'm only a newspaper hero.'

When Angus Murray, one of Taylor's henchmen – also described as a 'gentleman crook' by pliant Melbourne journalists – was sentenced to be hanged over the a murder of a Glenferrie bank manager in a robbery planned by Taylor, 70,000 people signed a petition calling for commutation of the death penalty. During a march through Melbourne streets by thousands of citizens, Taylor made an appearance in his car near Russell Street police headquarters and, 'like a potentate, returned the salute of numerous hands raised to caps as the protesters walked past'. It was, according to Hugh Anderson in *The Rise and Fall of Squizzy Taylor: Larrikin Crook*, the 'most spirited reprieve campaign since the clamour to save Ned Kelly in 1880'. Murray went to his death on the gallows in 1924, without implicating Taylor.

The untouched Taylor sought that same year to expand into Sydney, where cocaine trafficking was more profitable. Ironically, the police there made it too hard for him, with Taylor declaring on his return to Melbourne: 'The Sydney dees (detectives) are too hot. They're a bloody lot of narcs, and I'll let them have their harbour.' In his book, Hugh Anderson observed that Taylor 'preferred to stay in Melbourne, where he was generally tolerated'. So tolerated in fact that, after his return from Sydney, the wife of an ex-Governor of Victoria, Sir Arthur Stanley, was conned by a social worker into meeting Taylor at the Menzies Hotel. Flashily dressed, Taylor reportedly promised to make 'sincere and strenuous' efforts to change his ways. Taylor even sent Lady Stanley a silver jewel casket inscribed 'To one who understands from one misunderstood'.

So little influence did the lady have upon him that within months Taylor took to kidnapping young girls and turning them into drug addicts. One girl who disappeared, after being kidnapped by Taylor from a Frankston Hotel, was found abandoned a week later in a park, with an arm disfigured with needle marks from the wrist to the shoulder. As Hugh Anderson recorded, 'Girls were hooked on cocaine and then sent as pedlars for the men who safely supplied the pernicious traffic'.

Taylor was brought down not by the authorities but by another criminal.

He died after a shootout with a fellow drug dealer, John

'Snowy' Cutmore, in a house at Carlton on 27 October 1927. Cutmore also died. Cutmore had long been associated with Taylor and had run a particularly vicious standover gang known as the 'Safe Prosecution Gang', which stood over other criminals for their loot from safe robberies.

Taylor's funeral was described as a 'disgraceful exhibition of morbid curiosity'. It was at a time when Melbourne became known as a 'crime polluted city with a puritanical face'.

After Taylor's demise, Stokes assumed his mantle. He too was able to flourish unhindered, paying police to turn a blind eye to his two-up operations. In 1938, he introduced Australia's first illegal casino – operating night cruises around Port Phillip Bay in a refitted pilot boat, the *Alvina*. The following year he introduced illegal baccarat to Australia. The success of Stokes's baccarat school, especially during the Second World War, led to the establishment of similar baccarat operations in Sydney from 1945, which ultimately blossomed into fully-fledged casinos in the 1960s.

In his book *The Real John Wren*, in which he portrayed Wren as having been unfairly singled out and persecuted, Hugh Buggy complained that afterwards 'the most audacious and the most active underworld Melbourne has ever known grew up almost overnight like some giant toadstool'. Buggy wrote, 'But no meetings were called by the righteous to berate the underworld czar "Squizzy" Taylor, who, after a long and industrious apprenticeship, strutted the tawdry stage as the big-time crook. None of the voluble reformers called for prohibitive legislation when Henry Stokes in 1919 set up his elaborate two-up academy in Goodwood Street, Richmond. There were no platform fulminations when Stokes elevated two-up from a furtive backyard gamble to a social pleasantry to be enjoyed by more than the rabble behind a protective network of electronic bells and in settings of mounting elegance.

'Nor was the voice of the puritan heard many years later when Stokes invested baccarat with the veneer that lifted it in the social scale.

'Everywhere there was a strange silence, an apathy that was in marked contrast to the hysterical clamour against Wren's tote. There were drunken orgies in suburban beer houses. There were brawls and bashings and shootings almost nightly. There was scope for diversified gambling greater than Melbourne had ever known. And there was mass production vice flaunted brazenly on an expanding scale'. Melbourne, Buggy bemoaned, 'has always been a smug community preferring to believe that commercialised vice does not exist'.

Wren died in 1953 a wealthy man, by then prominent in a variety of legitimate business, including newspapers.

After the 1923 police strike, demands for a Royal Commission were headed off in the political arena, with Labor Party factions even pressing for reinstatement of sacked police.

One member of parliament, H. H. Smith, claimed there was 'no place on earth' where licensing police were 'so lax' with sly grog and two-up protected by police bribery. Smith was persuaded to desist with the appointment in 1925 of Brigadier General Sir Thomas Blamey as Chief Commissioner of Police lauded as an antidote to continuing corruption.

Apart from Squizzy Taylor and his ilk being able to continue to prosper, Blamey himself was soon to be accused of larrikinism, nepotism and bad judgement. He openly flouted licensing laws himself and allowed an open go for everybody.

Only weeks after Blamey took up his appointment, when three members of the licensing branch raided a brothel, a male client produced to them a police badge numbered '80', declaring: 'That is all right, boys. I am a plainclothes constable. Here is my badge.' It was Blamey's badge. Afterwards, Blamey claimed that the badge was 'surreptitiously' removed from his key ring two days previously and, just as mysteriously, returned to him two days after the raid. When a superintendent, Daniel Linehan, disputed the account, asserting that he had seen the badge on Blamey's desk late on the afternoon of the raid, he was criticised by the chief secretary as 'disloyal' and was forced to retire.

Subsequently the story was put about that Blamey had lent the badge to an out-of-town army friend, but still there remained those who believed that it was indeed Blamey himself who flashed the badge and that police had deliberately raided the brothel because they knew he was there – to get something on him as a hedge against him interfering with police rackets.

The open-go Blamey era lasted 11 years, withstanding constant calls for action against corruption. It ended after his chief of the CIB, John Brophy, was shot and wounded in mysterious circumstances at Royal Park on 22 May 1936. Blamey issued a statement claiming that Brophy had been shot while 'handling his revolver'. When it was disclosed that Brophy had been shot three times, in the right arm, cheek and above the heart, it was claimed he had been shot by bandits. Then it was disclosed that at the time Brophy had been seated in a chauffeur-driven Oldsmobile in the company of two women. The disclosures led to a Royal Commission, headed by Judge Hugh Macindoe, who found that Blamey had given 'replies which were not in accordance with the truth, with the sole purpose of secreting from the press the fact that women were in the company of Sup Brophy'. Blamey was forced to resign.

When an independent examination of the force was carried out by Alex Duncan of the United Kingdom's famous Flying Squad, it was reported, in polite British language, that detectives were 'not playing the game' and were 'free and easy'. In summary, the report noted 'serious allegations' against members of the force.

Further outsiders were to be brought in to run the force for more than a quarter of a century, without much changing, until after the legendary Henry Bolte took office as Premier.

2
The Bolte Era

When Henry Bolte took over as Premier of Victoria in 1955, he inherited a new Chief Commissioner of Police – along with an entrenched hotbed of police corruption. As Victoria's longest-serving Premier, Bolte managed to do probably less than most premiers in coming to grips with burgeoning crime and corruption, during a crucial period when old-style racketeering was making way for modern organised crime.

At the beginning of 1955, before Bolte became Premier, Selwyn Porter had already been appointed to succeed Alexander Duncan as Chief Commissioner of Police. Porter was to be the last of a succession of outsiders in the position.

Within a year, bribery allegations prompted Porter to order a clean-up of gaming squad police. The clean-up was so effective that it caused a shake-out in the control of the underworld, with criminal elements from the waterfront moving in to fill the void. When the then standover king Freddy 'The Frog' Harrison sought to exert influence over the new breed, he was executed in full view of dozens of people during a pay parade at 13 South Wharf. A gunman had walked up to Harrison, said, 'This is yours, Fred', and blasted half his head away with a 12-gauge shotgun. Historically, it was symbolic: all were to know that the now notorious painters and dockers were to be the new masters. In that shadowy world, an even more violent breed emerged, akin to gangsters of the New York waterfront – shooting first and asking questions later. Protected by a more rigid code of silence, as effective as any Italian mafia blood oath, they brooked no interference from outsiders.

Placed in charge of the clean-up was a young ex-army trooper, Mick Miller. Under him, the gaming squad became effective for the first time. Miller and his men became known as the 'Untouchables'. Miller's blitz preceded a Royal Commission that recommended legalisation of off-course totalisator betting – more than half a century after the shutdown of John Wren's infamous tote.

The Bolte Liberal Government thus introduced off-course betting, with the establishment of the Totalisator Agency Board in 1961. It was supposed to stamp out police corruption and wipe out illegal starting price (SP) betting. It achieved neither.

But Bolte did make a name for himself by steadfastly refusing to countenance legal poker machines, scores of thousands of which had been allowed in thousands of licensed clubs across the border in NSW. Bolte maintained poker machines had reduced the 'moral fibre' of NSW. Such utterances served to perpetuate Victoria's reputation as a wowser State.

In 1954, the year before Bolte became Premier, a Labor Government had introduced legal lotteries. The then Premier, Jack Cain, lured Tattersalls from its Tasmanian headquarters in Hobart to Melbourne, ostensibly to help pay for hospitals. Tattersalls had been in Tasmania since 1896. George Adams had first started his Tattersalls lotteries in Sydney in 1881. The lotteries were driven out of Sydney in 1893 by legislation that made them illegal. They were moved to Queensland where legislation again forced them out, and Adams shifted to Tasmania (later the first State to allow legal casinos). At that time, Victoria had declared it would never allow such an 'iniquitous evil'.

Jack Cain was known to everybody as 'Honest Jack', a

sobriquet to be bestowed on his son when he followed in his father's footsteps and became Premier of Victoria in 1982.

Jack Cain served as Premier for three periods – five days in 1943, two years from 1945 and three years from 1952. Though respected by Bolte as 'the greatest leader Labor ever had in this State', it was Bolte who took the credit for ousting him in 1955, by a landslide, in the wake of an ALP split precipitated by a no-confidence motion moved by Bolte as Opposition leader. Afflicted by outside and internal pressures to implement legislation favouring trade unions, the Cain administration was accused in Bolte's motion of accepting 'directions from sources which in the opinion of this House endanger the security of the country and the welfare of the State'. Nine Labor dissidents crossed the floor to vote with Bolte, bringing down the Government and leading to the formation of the right-wing Democratic Labor Party, which thereafter kept Bolte in power with its preferences.

A colourful, straight-talking sheep farmer who liked to call himself a country 'bumpkin', Bolte was able to mesmerise city crowds and country folk alike, as well as the upper echelons of Melbourne society, and served unchallenged for a record 17 years.

For a conservative State with a Victorian reputation, Bolte proved an ideal leader. He promoted Victoria as Australia's greatest State. As the traditional headquarters for British capital, Melbourne's financial status was at that time coming under threat from Sydney, which had become the main base for American and Japanese companies since the Second World War. In any case, the whole country was booming, Victoria along with it. Upon assuming power, Bolte could boast that only 338 people were drawing unemployment benefits in Victoria.

Discovery of gas in Bass Strait was to prove a bonanza for the State, and Bolte's political catchcries promised jobs for all, housing for everyone. His showpiece was the Victorian State Savings Bank, which was able to offer Government-guaranteed loans of the fair value of a home. Interest rates were five per cent, with no inflation.

On a more personal level, Bolte dictated the lifestyle of the period. Only after being in power for a decade did his administration allow people to attend the cinema on Sunday nights. Not until 1966 were hotel hours extended from six o'clock to 10 o'clock at night. Not until 1968 could football be played on Sundays. Not even Sunday newspapers were allowed until 1969.

An ardent free enterprise man, he presided over Victoria's most profitable era. Nobody quibbled when he received a knighthood. Though a mixer who usually knew what went on, everywhere, Sir Henry developed a public blind spot on crime and corruption.

A mad punter, his socialising at weekday and weekend race meetings epitomised the belief that racing was the sport of kings, without ever fully recognising its seamier side, and the endemic nature of ancillary betting rackets. Nor did he see anything wrong in using his patronage and power to assist his business mates.

In one parliamentary outburst, a Labor backbencher, Denis 'Dinny' Lovegrove, attacked Bolte's approach and philosophy for contributing towards making Victoria 'the centre for the biggest business takeovers in Australia today. It is the cockpit for all the most ruthless land sharks, usurers, profiteers, price riggers and commercial scoundrels that have ever infested the economic life of the country. Victoria is their utopia'.

It was also utopia for Calabrian criminal societies.

In Sydney, in 1956, the NSW commissioner of police, Colin Delaney, had adopted the unprecedented step of allowing media access to previously confidential police dossiers outlining the existence of ethnic Italian secret societies, then usually referred to as Black Hand cells. Commissioner Delaney's dossiers estimated that there were 70 to 80 members in Melbourne and 25 each in the Mildura and Shepparton districts in Victoria. Little interest was provoked in Victoria until seven years later when Victoria became the battleground for an outbreak of society violence.

In the early hours of 4 April 1963, a supposedly small-time market gardener, Vincenzo Angilletta, was blasted to death by a shotgun while parking his car in the garage at his home in the Melbourne suburb of Northcote. It was the start of a mafia power struggle that became known as the 'Melbourne Market Murders'. Rather than Black Hand, the now familiar term mafia rang around Australia. Predictably, police met a wall of silence.

Six months later, open warfare broke out, triggering a number of murders and woundings, the most significant being the killing of prominent markets merchant and commission agent Vincenzo Muratore, who was blasted with a shotgun outside his home in suburban Hampton.

Muratore had been a trusted lieutenant of Victorian mafia chief Domenico Italiano, known as 'The Pope', who had died in 1962. The Bolte administration reacted by calling in a mafia expert from America's Federal Bureau of Investigations, John Cusack, a key figure in smashing the fabled 'French Connection' narcotics network. With his help, several arrests were made.

Before returning to the United States, on 11 August 1964, Cusack presented a 25-page report to Victoria's Under Secretary John V. Dillon, detailing the existence in Melbourne, and elsewhere in Victoria, of an entrenched society known as 'the Honoured Society'. Or, in Calabrian parlance, L'Onorata or N'Dranghita. In summary, Cusack warned that within 25 years, mafia gangsters using strong-arm tactics would control or dominate a wide range of illegitimate and legitimate activities.

In his report, Cusack laid out a charter for Victoria to tackle organised crime on all fronts, a decade ahead of the initiation of any such moves in any other State police force. His report not only remained secret, but also was largely ignored. Twenty-five years later, during a further outbreak of mafia violence involving identities linked to the 'Market Murders' episode, the Melbourne *Age* lamented that what Cusack had predicted had by then come true.

In public terms, Bolte presented himself as an absolute law and order man – tough and brutal enough to sanction hanging.

Six years into the Bolte reign, on 8 August 1961, a woman aged 82, Edna Ethel Hall, widowed mother of a vicar, was murdered in horrible circumstances at All Saints' Vicarage at Hawthorn. She was slain by an alcoholic sexual psychopath, Robert Tait, who was looking for money. Tait struck the lady on the face, neck and chest, stripped off her underclothing and dragged her to a bed still 'moaning and breathing heavily' where Tait forced a torch into her vagina. She died from multiple injuries. Tait stole $15 in cash, a leather case and several pairs of women's pants.

Arrested, Tait was found guilty of murder in August 1962 and sentenced to be hanged. Not since 1952 had there been a hanging in Victoria. Opinion polls showed a majority in favour of hanging, not surprising since Victoria that year had recorded the highest number of murders in the nation. Nonetheless, there was a public furore to save Tait from the gallows, including opposition from the dead woman's own son. Opponents argued that Tait was insane and that it was illegal under common law to hang an insane person. The consulting psychiatrist with the NSW Department of Justice, Dr J. A. McGeorge, brought in by Victorian authorities, found Tait to be 'perfectly sane'. When the Bolte administration ordered the hanging to go ahead, the High Court intervened and ordered a reprieve a day before the due date, pending all legal avenues being exhausted. Within weeks, in the face of pressure from protesters, Bolte backed down, commuting Tait's sentence and committing him to the Ararat Mental Home. Bolte felt thwarted, handicapped by legal technicalities. He was pilloried by students as 'Henry the Hangman'.

A future editor of the *Age*, Creighton Burns, in a book, *The Tait Case*, observed that the Tait case 'provided a measure of the quality of the Victorian political system and of the way in which it operated'.

In dealing with general police and crime matters, Bolte relied on Arthur Rylah, his Chief Secretary and Attorney-General, who might well have been Premier himself but for the sudden downfall of the Cain administration. In fact, Bolte had been categorised as a 'stopgap' leader, with Rylah waiting in the wings until he could get the numbers to challenge him. Bolte was forever grateful, always allowing Rylah a free hand.

When Selwyn Porter died in office in 1963, Rylah recommended to Bolte the appointment of Rupert Arnold as Chief Commissioner, the first serving member of the force to be appointed to the top post since the historic police strike of 1923. Arnold endeared himself to factions of the force by promising 'no reforms'.

Richard Hall, in his book *Disorganised Crime*, raised the spectre that Arnold was corrupt. Hall mentioned Arnold's close relationship with one of Victoria's more notorious illegal gambling identities linked with gambling and drug interests in NSW.

Hall wrote: '... in retrospect the police now differ on whether or not the relationship was indiscreet or corrupt ...'.

In December 1965, an inquiry dubbed 'The Big Police Probe' was set up when a knockabout character, Brian Latch (who was to be referred to in the media as Mr X, Australia's famous police informer), made allegations of police corruption. In a book entitled simply *Mr X*, Bill Hitchings told of Latch being tracked down by GTV 9 newsreader Eric Pearce and reporter Michael Schildberger. Apparently amazed at what he heard, Pearce turned to Schildberger and asked: 'Does this sort of thing really go on, Michael? I expected this type of thing to go on in America, but not here in Australia.'

The inquiry was presided over by a magistrate sitting jointly with a police superintendent. In the inquiry, six police were charged with offences ranging from disgraceful and improper conduct to neglect and breach of duty. The charges were instituted by the State Solicitor, Mr Murray, resulting in demands by police for Murray to be sacked.

In the *Truth* newspaper, Sol Chandler commented: 'Any politician who likes to come forward and say that some people in the force want to set up a police state in Victoria now has ready-made evidence from the inside.'

After Latch had taken his evidence to Murray, Murray was recorded as saying, 'Remember this. I too can be run over by a train'.

According to Chandler, the Police Discipline Board 'leaned over backwards to be fair to the accused officers, and three men were found to be in default to a certain degree. Still mindful of police sensibilities, it would appear, the tribunal went so far as to ask one of the officers if its decision was okay by him'. All six accused officers were afterwards promoted. An exasperated Latch had maintained: 'I think a Royal Commission would be better.' Two officers who were relied upon to investigate his allegations were to be fingered and criticised some years later by another corruption inquiry.

During the same month that Latch had raised his allegations, another more memorable episode unfolded. A warder, George Hodson, was shot dead during an escape from Pentridge prison by Ronald Ryan and Peter Walker.

In December 1966, after Ryan had been convicted, it was announced that Cabinet had decided Ryan should be hanged. When protests erupted, Bolte asserted: 'There is no possibility of the decision to hang Ryan being reversed. It is quite definite and final. We have done what we believe is right. This decision has not been taken lightly. We knew the press would oppose it. We knew those groups which are protesting would protest.'

Ryan lost an appeal to the Privy Council. Feeling was abroad that Bolte wanted to hang Ryan in revenge for having been thwarted in the Tait case. Marchers stormed Parliament House. Eight thousand demonstrated outside Pentridge, many brandishing placards that read: HANG BOLTE.

A stay of execution was granted by Justice Starke, based on an affidavit by an ex-prisoner, John Henry Tolmie, suggesting that Ryan might not have fired the shot that killed the warder. Tolmie was arrested for perjury when it was discovered he was not at Pentridge at the time. As Peter Blazey recorded in a biography of Bolte, 'after the discrediting of Tolmie, resistance ended'.

As Bolte explained in *Bolte by Bolte*, a book written with Tom Prior, 'The more the media used propaganda and publicity to save Ryan, the tighter they were tying the knot around his neck. It was a confrontation the Government simply could not afford to back away from; it would have lost all credibility if it had'.

Ryan was hanged on 3 February 1967 – the last person to be hanged in Australia.

Three thousand protesters gathered outside the jail gates on the previous evening, booing and chanting. When the Labor Party sought to use the capital punishment issue four months later in an election, it backfired and Bolte gained six more seats.

Beneath the shadow of such a tough law and order administration, police were given free reign to deal with demonstrators during anti-Vietnam War rallies in the late 1960s and early 1970s. After the first violent confrontation outside the United States Consulate on 4 July 1968, Chief Commissioner Arnold denounced protesters as 'so-called intellectuals who want to change the world' and suggested it would be a 'simple matter to drop them on uninhabited desert islands'. Moreover, warning against demonstrations in public places, he proclaimed: 'So long as I am Chief Commissioner ... I require it to be crushed in its incipient stages with all the force necessary.'

In contrast, elements within police ranks were able to operate with impunity.

In mid-1969, an abortion law reformer, Dr Bertram Wainer, raised allegations of police corruption in protecting backyard abortionists. Indeed, police were protecting various rackets, including illegal gambling and prostitution, no differently than what was known to be going on in more notorious NSW.

When Wainer, a member of the Abortion Law Reform Association, first spoke up, he was met with political and media indifference.

Not until Wainer received assistance from journalist Evan Whitton and his wife Noela did anything really happen. A scholarly writer, Whitton then wrote for *Truth*, to which he turned after failing to get a job with the *Age*.

In pursuing the corrupt network nominated by Wainer, Whitton was to earn distinction as the pioneer of modern investigative journalism, in forcing the first judicial inquiry into police corruption in modern times. Later the editor of the *National Times* and chief reporter for the *Sydney Morning Herald*, Whitton was to win four more Walkley Awards and write a number of bestselling books on crime and corruption.

With help from the Whittons, Wainer produced affidavits setting out full details of police graft involving abortionists – alleging senior police had been copping bribes for more than 20 years to protect illegal abortionists against police raids. It was an early arm of modern organised crime.

When Evan Whitton's disclosures were published in *Truth*, other sections of the media began to take up the issue. A tape of a news briefing given by Bolte at the time, as disclosed in the Peter Blazey book, typified the outlook of the Government of the day. Bolte was asked whether he had seen Wainer on television the night before (15 December 1969).

Bolte: 'Naw! He's pathetic! He's probably certifiable ... I'm told he was involved in that $10 note forgery case recently. Who was it? ... Anyway, they used his house. Now that's rather interesting. I think we could make some use of that ...'.

Nearly a week beforehand, on 9 December, a series of affidavits had been handed to the Solicitor-General, Basil Murray, QC. They alleged that police were protecting doctors as well as backyard abortionists, including Charles Wyatt, a former Victorian policeman.

During the six months since Wainer had originally complained, one of the police officers running the racket, Jack Ford, was promoted to chief of the homicide squad, the very bastion of the graft network.

On Christmas Day, when Victorians were least likely to be interested in such matters, Chief Secretary Rylah made a statement seeking to bury the Wainer allegations as 'completely unfounded', saying a police report was inconclusive. On 3 January 1970, when the issue was finally pursued by the *Age*, the Government caved in. On 5 January, an inquiry was ordered, headed by William Kaye, QC. It unravelled allegations of systematic graft dating back to 1953, two years before the Bolte regime ousted Jack Cain's administration.

As a result, Jack Mathews, superintendent; and Jack Ford, inspector, were jailed for five years; and Martin Jacobson, a senior constable, was jailed for three years. They were described by Crown Prosecutor Norman O'Brien, QC, as 'avaricious parasites'. When sentencing them, Justice Starke commented, 'By your conduct you have severely shaken the community's confidence in the Victoria Police Force, and inevitable I think the morale of the Force itself must have been lowered'.

Describing the saga as 'one of the most sensational and controversial public inquiries and criminal trials this State has ever experienced', the *Age* editorialised: 'It would be naive to suppose that responsible Ministers and officials, and successive police chiefs, could have had no inkling of what was going on.'

Jack Mathews, the more senior of the pack, was allowed to retire gracefully so that he could collect full taxpayer contributions to his pension, though he failed to perform the job for which taxpayers had paid his salary. On his own evidence, he admitted that, in five years as head of the homicide squad, he had not arrested a single abortionist.

Mathews, of all people, had been put in charge of the Mr X inquiries. About the same time, following a series of mafia murders linked with the Melbourne markets, Victoria was invited to send a senior policeman to the United States for a three-month study tour with the Federal Bureau of Investigations. Mathews was nominated but stood aside in favour of Jack Ford. In America, Ford was supposed to study how to combat organised crime. On his return, Ford concentrated on widening his own graft network, as revealed by Peggy Berman, one-time girlfriend of Ford and a key inside witness for the Kaye inquiry and in the trials against Mathews, Ford and others, in her book *Why Isn't She Dead!*, produced with journalist Kevin Childs. The book detailed how Mathews was then also appointed as officer in charge of complaints against police, reporting direct to Chief Commissioner Arnold. In Berman's account, Mathews told her, 'They come in here, dear, and I give them a good, sympathetic hearing. When they go I just screw up the paper and throw it in the waste-paper basket'.

Berman disclosed that Ford talked to her about judges, lawyers and Crown Law Department officials being part of the protection system. Significantly, inside friends of the corrupt policemen sought to sabotage criminal proceedings against them: 36 Kaye inquiry exhibits went missing.

In *The People's Force*, police historian Robert Haldane observed: 'Many people did not accept the simplistic notion that all was basically well within the force except for the activities of a few "rotten apples".' As Haldane commented, 'The concern expressed by the *Age* and others that something was seriously wrong with the force was well founded. It was not limited to police corruption or illegal behaviour, however. The rot undermining the force included these taints, but they existed largely because the force was suffering from a more general and complex combination of political neglect, public apathy, maladministration, demoralisingly low pay and sub-standard work benefits'. Haldane wrote that their pay was 'not sufficient to place them above the sort of common temptations offered by SP bookmakers, hoteliers trading after hours and shopkeepers wanting special favours'.

On 26 March 1971, a criminal, Neil Collingburn, was injured after being taken into custody for questioning over a set of golf clubs. He died two days later. The golf clubs turned out to be his own. Two police were suspended and charged with manslaughter. Their subsequent acquittal became a cause célèbre. Demonstrations were staged in the city. Waterside workers went on strike.

Nobody in authority, least of all Bolte or Rylah, would

acknowledge that there might be continuing problems within the police force. It was a regular occurrence for Rylah, the minister, to liaise with Jack Mathews, the homicide man. According to veteran police reporter Alan Dower in his book *Deadline*, Rylah had very close liaison through critical times with Chief Commissioner Arnold, but 'had engineered and groomed an even closer working relationship and personal bond with Mathews'. Wrote Dower: 'No other person knew of their meetings at this time. Never were the two seen together at Parliament House, at the Chief Secretary's suite in the Old Treasury Building in Spring Street, at Russell Street headquarters. To avoid being shadowed or overheard, over many weeks they met only on Saturday afternoons at the Caulfield, Flemington and Moonee Valley racecourses.' It was during such meetings, wrote Dower, that Rylah and Mathews devised strategy to investigate the 'Market Murders'.

In retrospect, the influence of Rylah cannot be underestimated. He was minister in charge of the police from 1955 until 1971. Suspicion persisted that Rylah may have been compromised because of the manner in which police handled inquiries surrounding the death of his wife on 15 March 1969, only months before Wainer made his allegations.

In *Can of Worms II*, Evan Whitton, disclosing that Wainer had first offered his evidence to Rylah, surmised: 'Rylah, risking a charge of perverting the course of justice by failure to properly investigate a crime, refused to accept the evidence. His excuse was that he owed the homicide squad a debt of gratitude for the courtesy and consideration shown to him over the mysterious death – never yet adequately explained – of his wife.'

Rylah had been living away from his wife. After her body was found, a Sydney Sunday newspaper reported she had been shot. She died on Saturday morning and no death certificate was signed for her. A post-mortem was held on the

Saturday afternoon and a coroner ordered her cremation within three days, without holding an inquest. According to Rylah, she had died of a cerebral hemorrhage, having inexplicably left her house to go into the cold of early morning.

In the midst of the abortion scandal, the Bolte regime faced an election. Wainer threw his hat into the ring by standing against Rylah in his blue-ribbon seat of Kew.

On the eve of the election, his efforts to expose corruption in Victoria were rewarded with headlines calculated to down him. Newspapers picked up the closing statements of John Winneke, junior counsel for the Kaye inquiry. On its front page on the Friday afternoon, the Melbourne *Herald* headlined: IT'S OVER – WAINER EVIDENCE DISCREDITS HIM – WINNEKE. The *Sun News-Pictorial* followed up next morning: WINNEKE: WAINER A GRANDSTANDER. Wainer still got a creditable 14 per cent of the votes. In just over eight months, Rylah resigned. When Rylah later collapsed and died, Bolte wept.

Rylah had always promoted a puritanical image. Once, when addressing the Sacred Heart School in his electorate of Kew, he had proclaimed: 'We have got to provide an alternative to sex in the lives of our children and in the lives of the community.' At Parliament House, he displayed a preoccupation with pornography, often displaying imported magazines to journalists in his office, pouring over them while uttering objection to them.

Bolte, too, exuded an aura of self-righteousness. Before his death on 4 January 1990, Bolte recalled for Tom Prior in *Bolte by Bolte* a meeting with Sir Robert Askin, Bolte's Liberal counterpart in NSW, who was found to have been corrupt: 'I was in Sydney once and made a courtesy call to his office,' related Bolte. 'He asked me if I had a "good thing" at the races and, as it happened, I had. I told him the name of the horse, and he immediately made a phone call and placed a heavy bet, heavy by my standards, anyway. Askin told me he was betting with his SP bookmaker. It was embarrassing, but what could I do? I think the horse won, but I didn't give Askin any more tips. I wouldn't have done a thing like that in a million years in Victoria.'

When Sir Robert Askin, and Queensland politicians, came under fire in 1970 for accepting an allotment of shares in Comalco Ltd, in advance of Comalco joining public listing, it was found that Sir Henry, too, had accepted some. Beforehand, in Melbourne, the shares had been unofficially traded at $3.50 before listing. Askin, Bolte and almost the entire Queensland Cabinet were handed theirs for $2.75, when they expected to start at about $4 on the public market. While the others took 1500 shares each (at a profit of $1.25 each), Sir Henry settled for 333 for himself and 166 for his wife. Sir Arthur Rylah got 101. Their credibility remained intact.

During his retirement, Sir Henry, then 75, was involved in a motor accident outside the gate of his farm 'Kialla' at Banganie on 24 March 1984. He ended up in hospital with a broken leg, a fractured breast bone and bruising. Hospital blood samples showed that he had a blood alcohol reading above the legal limit of .05, a law he had enacted. There was media speculation that he would have to be charged. Inexplicably, however, the blood samples were replaced by a sample showing less than .05.

'I remember,' Bolte confided to Tom Prior, 'having a few drinks that afternoon; I usually do, but not many, not many, and I don't tell lies. I don't know what happened to the bloody blood samples. How could I? I was in intensive care, only bloody semi-conscious, for three weeks.' Prior suggested that, 'understandably, if not quite legally', Sir Henry was allowed 'one for the road'. On stepping down as Premier in 1972, Bolte had been so confident of the dynasty he had created that he predicted the Liberals would rule in Victoria for another decade. He was right.

3

The Hamer Days

When Dick Hamer took over as Premier of Victoria from Henry Bolte in 1972, all was not rosy in the Garden State. The manifestations of organised crime were conspicuously evident – with continuing feuding among the Melbourne painters and dockers over the spoils from organised crime rackets.

From across the border in NSW, where the administration of Sir Robert Askin was coming under scrutiny over its patronage of organised crime and police corruption, Sydney's 'Mr Big', Lennie McPherson, gave a media interview in which he portrayed Melbourne as being worse than Sydney. 'Down there,' he said, 'they run hot.' As McPherson put it, he would not go near the place for a million quid.

In the lead-up to an election for the maverick Federated Ship Painters and Dockers' Union, the warfare reached its zenith. Alfred 'The Ferret' Nelson, officially the union welfare officer, disappeared. Although his car was fished from 10 metres of water near a wharf, his body was never found. Within days, Desmond 'Cossie' Costello was murdered in reprisal. His body was dumped in an excavation ditch near Collingwood. On election day, one painter and docker, Jimmy Bazley, stood with a gun in his hand and a foot on the ballot box. Nobody was hit or admitted seeing anything when seven bullets were fired into the South Melbourne union office. Bazley was to be wounded, twice, in subsequent ambushes; he told police nothing. In the toing and froing, there were more victims and disappearances. Nobody talked.

Terry Gordon, the union's federal secretary, suggested there was nothing unusual about the violence: 'Is this unusual? I know managing directors who have got shot, wharfies who have got shot, people in all walks of life who have got shot. What is happening within the union is the union's own affair and will be settled by the union.' It was Gordon who told an earlier federal inquiry into the waterfront: 'We catch and kill our own.'

Frustrated, the chief of the homicide squad, Kevin Carton, prepared a report and appealed to the Government for a Victorian judicial inquiry. The Government declined.

As if playing to Victorian officialdom's mentality of 'out of sight, out of mind', Patrick Shannon, union secretary, boasted that 'no stray bullet or bomb has harmed a non-union member'. Yet 15 months later, when a gunman rushed into the Moonee Valley Hotel in Fitzroy, killing docker Laurence Chamings in a spray of bullets, also killed was a boy aged 10, Nicholas Kolovrat. Then Shannon himself was gunned to death in the Druid's Hotel, South Melbourne, in October 1973.

The outgunned presidential candidate in the union election, Bill 'The Texan' Longley, was convicted of Shannon's murder. Earlier, Longley had been convicted for playing a part in an excursion by Victorians into NSW to pull off the infamous $587,870 Mayne Nickless armoured van robbery in the Sydney suburb of Guildford on 4 March 1970. It was then the biggest hold-up in Australia's history.

In October 1974, the Hamer administration was to be haunted by a resurrection of the crusading zeal of abortion law reformer, Dr Bertram Wainer. This time, he brought forward fresh allegations that more police were guilty of illegal behaviour. Wainer presented a file to the Solicitor-General, Daryl Dawson. Hamer reacted quicker than the

Bolte–Rylah regime might have. A preliminary investigation by Cairns Villeneuve-Smith led to a full-scale inquiry under Barry Beach, QC. Although a total of 131 complaints were made, Beach concentrated on inquiring into 21 of them. As it was, the investigation took 15 months. Beach made adverse findings against 55 police for a variety of offences, including receiving money corruptly, conspiracy, assault, unlawful arrest, perjury and fabricating evidence. Beach also recommended belated reforms.

Without even waiting for the tabling of the report, police unrest erupted on a scale not threatened since the Victorian police strike of 1923. At that same time, allegations were being raised in a push for a clean-up of institutionalised corruption in the police force in neighbouring NSW. In comparison, however, the Beach inquiry had revolved largely around allegations of police heavy-handedness in pursuing criminals. As inexcusable as their methods might have been, it pointed to overzealousness more than outright corruption.

After Rupert Arnold had retired as Chief Commissioner in 1969, Noel Wilby served for two years, before Reg Jackson was appointed in 1971, the year before Sir Henry Bolte retired as Premier.

In the face of the Beach probe, Jackson took to the podium to defend his force. At a Victorian Police Association mass meeting, he was given a standing ovation. It was hailed by president L. J. Blogg as the greatest demonstration of unity in the history of the association. Police talked of strike action, but resorted to work to rule. Premier Hamer wilted. Only 32 out of the 55 police cited were charged. Not one was convicted. Most were subsequently promoted, some to senior posts.

A review committee was set up to consider Beach recommendations for reform. The committee – headed by a former judge, J. G. Norris, and including Reg Jackson, and two others, R. Glenister and R. L. King – opted for the status quo.

According to Robert Haldane in *The People's Force*, 'Criticism of the final outcome of the Beach Inquiry was justified. It was a result that defied commonsense ... The corrupt, unlucky and stupid – and all who came near those categories – were gathered under the one umbrella and sheltered ... The force displayed a reluctance to admit to, or cleanse itself of, undesirable elements and was reactionary in its resistance to Beach's recommendations for reform ... Lawyers and magistrates played key parts in determining the outcome of prosecutions recommended by Beach and, because of their participation in the legal process, policemen alone could not be blamed for the results. However, more troubling than the possibility that a few crooked policemen might have gone unpunished was the bitter public after taste that policemen had displayed a "collective assumption" that they were "beyond reproach and above the law".'

That all was not well in Victoria was graphically brought home when a high-ranking member of a sister agency, Ian Ramsay Brown, head of the Melbourne office of the Federal Bureau of Narcotics, was secretly taped between 2 May 1975 and 24 September 1975. Subsequently, Brown was imprisoned for 12 years for drug trafficking. It was Australia's first public awakening to the extent of corruption in the drug trade.

When Jackson retired, in the wake of the Beach episode, Hamer, to his credit, acted to pull Victorian police into line and restore public confidence. Fortuitously, he selected Mick Miller, who was to prove the finest Chief Commissioner in the entire history of the State.

On taking office in 1977, Miller declared that 'nobody was above the law' and warned that, where police conduct was clearly unsatisfactory or where there was clearly a breach of law, it was 'unrealistic to suggest that the member should be supported'.

Since initiation of the Wainer crusade eight years previously, police brotherhood attitudes had become more entrenched, with the Victorian Police Association paying for the legal defence of any police charged with indictable offences. It had not been the case before. Miller's appointment did not suit the association, which engineered a no-confidence motion against him. Undeterred, Miller embarked on reforms eclipsing any hitherto attempted.

Miller had impressed Hamer when Hamer had been appointed Chief Secretary of Victoria by Henry Bolte, to succeed Sir Arthur Rylah on his retirement in 1971. Hamer had convened a meeting between police and protest groups to formulate acceptable guidelines for demonstrations to avoid further confrontation. Miller had just been promoted to assistant commissioner in charge of operations, which meant he had responsibility for police control of demonstrations. His approach was that, in controlling demonstrations, police should operate low-key rather than confront protesters. Rarely afterwards did demonstrations lead to unprovoked violence.

Under Miller, the force underwent a transformation. An intelligent, no-nonsense administrator, Miller over the following decade stamped on any signs of malpractice or corruption. It was an attitude that permeated to the most junior ranks. Under his reign, the Victorian force was continually referred to as Australia's premier force – even though there were still subtle and dangerous elements within.

The year of Miller's appointment as Chief Commissioner marked the beginning of Australia-wide outrage over organised crime and corruption following the assassination of anti-drug crusader Donald Mackay at Griffith, NSW, on 15 July 1977. Victorians looked askance at NSW, where an embarrassed Labor Premier, Neville Wran, was forced to order a Royal Commission. Apart from focusing on drug rackets in Sydney and at Griffith, the commission unearthed connections in Melbourne.

While the commission was holding hearings in NSW into Mackay's assassination, Monash University students in Victoria planned to mark the anniversary of Mackay's murder by staging a 'memorial'. Their treatment was to take the form of a musical comedy, using a Donald Mackay look-alike. When Mackay's widow, Barbara, publicly denounced the student plan as 'rather sick' and in 'extremely poor taste', the students were embarrassed into apologising.

What the NSW commission did not find out at the time was that mafia bosses who ordered Mackay's murder had turned to Melbourne not Sydney for execution of the conspiracy. Drug boss Bob Trimbole, who started his crime career servicing illegal poker machines in Victoria, contacted Melbourne mafia identity Gianfranco Tizzoni, a drug trafficker and police informant. Tizzoni enlisted Melbourne gunsmith George Joseph, patron of the Victoria Police Pistol Club, to arrange a hit man. Joseph had popped up during the Kaye inquiry into Wainer's allegations, with Kaye accepting Joseph as a witness of truth and taking the view that Wainer had been guilty of a flight of fancy in describing him as a member of the underworld. Through Joseph, Tizzoni allegedly recruited painter and docker Jimmy Bazley to carry out the assassination. Along with Tizzoni and Joseph, Bazley was ultimately convicted of conspiracy to murder Mackay and sentenced to life imprisonment. Both Tizzoni and Joseph received sweetheart deals and were out of jail in a short time.

One of Miller's early moves had been to appoint Fred Silvester to establish a proper Bureau of Criminal Intelligence (BCI). Without fear or favour, Silvester ordered operations against organised crime on all fronts, especially against Calabrian criminal societies neglected since the pigeonholing of the Cusack report during the Bolte administration.

It was the bureau that Silvester established that caught up with Tizzoni and provided the breakthrough in solving the Mackay murder.

In 1984, when Trimbole was arrested in Ireland, efforts to extradict him to Australia failed largely because of the efforts of British constitutional lawyer Patrick MacEntree, fond of defending IRA terrorists. When MacEntree later visited Australia, he was feted in Melbourne at the Australian Legal Convention.

By tackling corruption within the force, and targeting organised crime without, especially with the use of task forces, Miller lifted public confidence in the police, so much that opinion polls rated police fourth in Victoria among 15 professions in terms of honesty and ethical standards – above politicians, lawyers, accountants, university lecturers and school teachers.

Out of the Wainer saga, acknowledged Robert Haldane, grew the fruits of reform. In all, 15 Royal Commissions and other inquiries had been held into police from 1839 to 1984 – and the force was all the better because of them.

Reform in another context was used as an excuse when a Labor backbencher, Dolph Eddy, a former mayor of Collingwood, came under attack in 1978 over involvement with one of the criminal stars of the Beach inquiry – Peter Lawless. Sentenced to life imprisonment for murdering a man at Noble Park in 1973, Lawless claimed before Beach that he had been set up by police. When the Beach report 'cast doubts on the propriety of Lawless's conviction', Eddy supported Lawless in demands for a retrial. This was rejected by the State Full Court, as well as the High Court, although one High Court judge, Justice Lionel Murphy, dissented, saying Lawless had been denied a full and fair trial.

In November 1978, it was revealed in Parliament that plans for a new prison remand centre had been found in

Lawless's cell at Pentridge jail. Photocopies of the plans had been given earlier to Dolph Eddy at a briefing. Also found were six books borrowed by Eddy from the parliamentary library. Two days later, Eddy was attacked over having provided a reference for criminal Lance Chee, who had been sentenced that week to more than 15 years' jail for armed robbery and car theft.

In 1962, before entering Parliament, Eddy had resigned as a Justice of the Peace after being criticised by a judge over an affidavit involving three men and a woman subsequently jailed for conspiracy. Judge Gunson described as 'bizarre and reprehensible' Eddy's action in witnessing the swearing of the false affidavit. In response, the Chief Secretary, Sir Arthur Rylah, said the matter had been investigated and that he was satisfied with Eddy's resignation. Five years later, Eddy was reinstated as a JP.

After the Lawless episode, Eddy was dumped from Labor Party pre-selection for the following State election, in favour of barrister Jim Kennan, who was to become Attorney-General and Deputy Premier in a future Labor Government. Eddy's farewell at the Prince Alfred Hotel in Richmond was attended by painters and dockers, waterside and council workers and priests, all singing 'For he's a jolly good fellow'. Eddy died in 1989.

Suspicion of police connivance in aiding with inside knowledge of court security arose following the dramatic murder on 12 November 1979 of Raymond 'Chuck' Bennett in the Melbourne City Court building opposite Russell Street police headquarters. Bennett was gunned down while being led by police into the court to face robbery charges. As deadly as NSW criminals could be, none had dared intrude into court precincts to murder someone.

Bennett had been acquitted two years earlier of murdering Les Kane, and Bennett's murder was believed to have been masterminded by Kane's brother, Brian, with possible help from friendly police. During the trial of Bennett, Kane's widow, Judith, said he had been shot by silenced machine guns in the bathroom of their house after she had been pushed out of the way into another room. 'There's going to be revenge,' she said. 'Not only from his family, but a lot of other people.'

The fearsome Kanes had become the dominant force in protection rackets, collecting money from Chinese gambling houses and a two-up school. Brian Kane, nominated as the then mastermind of organised crime in Melbourne, was shot dead in a Brunswick Hotel two years later. More than 500 people attended his funeral. His gambling collection racket was taken over by a young Italian gangster with ambitions of becoming the Al Capone of Melbourne.

Bennett had been a suspect in Melbourne's 'Big Bookie Robbery' of 21 April 1976, when a gang got away with an undisclosed sum, reputedly as much as $6 million, on 'settling day' at the Victorian Club. It became not only Australia's biggest robbery, but also the first in which machine-guns were used.

Concern over the Bennett killing, and major revelations about organised crime tentacles emanating from NSW, spurred a group of backbench Liberals to push for establishment of a crime commission in Victoria. One had been recommended for NSW, but had been rejected by Neville Wran.

Not only did Hamer also resist the concept for Victoria, but also further upset both parliamentary and grassroots party supporters by proposing the establishment in Melbourne of a legal casino.

A group of backbench Liberals got together and assembled an extraordinary 28-page report purporting to outline the 'key structure of organised crime in Australia'. It blandly named some of Australia's political leaders, richest businessmen, high-ranking public servants and trade union leaders. In a nutshell, the report was a nonsense. Incredibly, for a Victorian-based report, it somehow managed not to identify any underworld figure actually involved in any of the State's blatantly obvious rackets.

The report relied heavily on anonymous American sources, which painted a picture of Victorian politicians and other figures being in the grip of a mafia takeover from the United States. In reality, the report's compilers were hoaxed. Again, not one mafia figure involved with Victoria was mentioned.

Little did they realise that at the time, American organised crime figures were suppliers of hard-core pornography, which was tolerated in Victoria under the Liberal regime. Norman Arno, ringleader of America's biggest pornography racket, visited Victoria in March 1980, liaising with a Melbourne identity, Alexander Gajic, a video porn distributor also nominated by the NSW Woodward Royal Commission as 'a principal member, in Melbourne, of an interstate heroin distribution group'. Having just been arrested by the FBI in a crackdown on a $4 billion racket, Arno actually went back to court to have bail conditions relaxed so that he could travel to Australia. As queried by an FBI agent, 'What could be so important, or so big in Australia, to demand such urgent attention when a billion dollar business was on the line back in America?'

One of Arno's lieutenants, Theodore Gaswirth, also officially listed by United States authorities as an organised crime figure, visited Melbourne twice in 1981. Also that year a business was established in Melbourne by Louis Esposito, a well documented crime figure associated with mafia expansion in Florida and California. He was able to visit Melbourne while wanted for gangland murders in New York.

Indeed, the New York mafia boss fictionalised for Mario Puzo's book *The Godfather*, Carlo Gambino, was negotiating for an interest in a gambling venture in Victoria. Gambino had been courted by Jeffrey Leo Patterson, who that year engaged in an ill-fated attempt to become president of Fitzroy Football Club. A telegram from Gambino to Patterson recovered by police read: 'Will finance your poker project fully to half million US dollars for fifty per cent your share.'

As an agent for American suppliers in the poker machine business, Patterson had had the benefit of impressive credentials for his overseas dealings. In October 1978, he obtained a State Government credential issued by Premier Hamer on representations from MLC Dolph Eddy. Of course, any government can find itself in an embarrassing position of having given a government imprimatur to individuals whose background may not be known.

However much it missed the real marks, the report by Liberal backbenchers, dated 25 February 1980, caused a stir when circulated in political and police circles. It related as fact a rumour that a political leader was 'compromised over a film relating to his extracurricular activities while overseas'. The report did acknowledge that 'domestic sources' were in some conflict over the existence of the film, but stated that American sources were adamant that the film had existed, although they had lost track of it. No such film was found to exist. Such conjecture precipitated an upheaval within the Hamer administration, which continued to oppose establishment of a State crime commission. However, in a concluding section, the report did recommend establishment instead of a national crime commission, a proposition that was taken up federally and influenced the then Liberal Prime Minister, Malcolm Fraser, a Victorian, in deciding to set up such a national body.

In the meantime, Fraser ordered the historic Royal Commission into the Federated Painters and Dockers' Union presided over by Frank Costigan, QC, triggered, ironically, by the breaking of their code of silence by none other than Bill Longley. Languishing in Pentridge, and proclaiming his innocence of the Shannon murder, Longley gave a startling interview to journalist David Richards. Published in the *Bulletin* in March 1980 as part of an exclusive series on painter and docker murder and mayhem, Richards's disclosures had such an effect around Australia that Fraser decided to act.

Fearing reprisals against Richards, Mick Miller took the unprecedented step of allowing Richards to carry a pistol.

The Costigan commission found that all 11 serving office holders in the union's Victorian branch had criminal records, with a total of 251 convictions recorded against them. Called as a witness, Longley claimed between 30 and 40 men had been killed in struggles for control of the union and its rackets in less than 15 years following the 1958 murder of old-time racket boss Freddie Harrison. Costigan reported that the code of silence had operated so successfully that only one conviction had been recorded among all the murders: that of Longley over the murder of Shannon. On the morning that Shannon's successor as secretary, Jack 'Putty Nose' Nicholls, was to have given evidence under summons over Shannon's murder, his body was found in his car 273 kilometres from Melbourne on the Hume Highway – shot through the head, with a suicide note alongside.

In November 1980, two months after the Costigan commission had started, allegations were made to the Victorian police internal affairs section alleging corruption among members of the gaming squad. Eleven months later, coinciding with Costigan inquiries that led to links with illegal starting price bookmaking, a police task force was established, code-named Operation Zebra. It resulted in a purge against 18 police. The end result was that only one was convicted, one acquitted, five disciplined by the Police Discipline Board, four discharged on medical grounds and two reprimanded. No criminal or disciplinary charges were laid against a further five. However, the task force operation did result in 550 arrests of others, with court fines exceeding $1 million. The whole operation was kept secret – until leaked to the *Age* in October 1984.

Recalling that he had headed a similar task force in a clean-up in the 1950s, Mick Miller said he could not guarantee there would not be more corruption in the future. 'No guarantee other than constant vigilance, and the introduction of safeguards and auditing procedures in an endeavour to ensure that it does not happen. But one can't legislate for human nature.'

The Costigan commission opened a veritable Pandora's box. Painters and dockers were found to have been used by promoters and businessmen to front as sham directors of companies stripped of their assets to evade tax. According to the Commonwealth Treasury, tax losses totalled $1.5 billion. Dubbed bottom-of-the-harbour schemes, a company variation of a term usually used to denote the dumping of bodies, the rackets pointed up a convenient nexus between the underworld and the so-called upperworld of society.

Melbourne had been more used to manifestations of that in suburban fiefdoms, a hangover of old-time, Tammany-Hall conduct of municipal affairs in inner suburbs such as Richmond. People delivering literature for opposition candidates were beaten. Cars were firebombed and house windows smashed. Teams went about removing from letterboxes newspapers containing any material favourable to opposition candidates. On election days, at polling booths, opposition how-to-vote cards were grabbed from the hands of supporters and burned.

In the ultimate, dead men voted. When people died, or moved to another suburb, their names were left on electoral rolls. Voter impersonation and multiple voting became commonplace. When authorities managed to convict an employee of Richmond council in 1975 for voting twice under another name, colleagues took up a collection to pay his $1500 fine and he was welcome to keep his job with the council. Ruling Labor Party factions went out of their way to encourage postal voting, then intercepted the mail to substitute votes with false ballot papers. When opposing candidates still managed to get enough votes, they suddenly found themselves 'unelected' following recounts, where seals on ballot boxes were broken and false votes substituted. Rarely did State authorities intervene. In 1978, after a Liberal backbencher, Morrie Williams, presented a petition to Parliament demanding an inquiry into alleged bribery in Richmond council, police reported that they could not substantiate the allegations.

In 1981, an independent candidate, Andrew Alexander, did his own detective work, and obtained statutory declarations from 14 people who swore they had cast postal ballots for a candidate who had been credited with just five postal votes. An electoral officer also reported having counted 11 more ballots than he had issued. On July 1981, the Liberal Government finally announced a judicial inquiry, headed by Alastair Nicholson, QC.

Meanwhile, a far bigger scandal had been brewing against the Liberal Party. In a new approach to public housing, Hamer, soon after taking over from Bolte in 1972, adopted a concept of satellite towns on the outskirts of Melbourne. The Housing Commission of Victoria began buying up large tracts of land. By 1974, it had spent more than $10 million to buy 1350 hectares. In scenes reminiscent of the late 19th century land boom days, speculators moved in first and bought up land on the fringes of the metropolis. They later sold it to commission for windfall profits. In one instance, a finance company bought one parcel of land at Sunbury for less than $2 million and sold it to commission on the very same day for nearly $3.5 million. Not only was taxpayers' money being squandered, but also the profiteering inflated all land prices and fuelled inflation.

As outlined by P. N. Grabosky in *Wayward Governance*, allegation were raised of patently incompetent management, and corruption.

This first public hint of the scandal, which bedevilled the Hamer administration for seven years, had come with an 'Insight' exposé by Ben Hills and Phillip Chubb in the *Age* in June 1974. Shortly beforehand, the private secretary to the Minister for Planning had been advised that somebody within the Housing Commission was receiving questionable payments. The secretary, Geoffrey Underwood, advised the office of the Minister for Housing. No action was taken.

Later that year, when renewed allegations were made, an assistant commissioner of police, Bill Crowley, was appointed to investigate. Within a week, Crowley had disposed of the allegations, recommending: 'Indeed, any extension of the inquiry at this stage would almost certainly extend current rumours and play into the hands of journalists and others who have recently been making further inquiries.'

Three years later, when two Liberal backbenchers abstained when the Labor Opposition moved a vote of no-confidence against the Hamer administration, they were expelled from the Liberal Party. In the resulting furore, the Government was pressured into ordering a board of inquiry, headed by a former Supreme Court judge, Sir Gregory Gowans. It recommended charges against a Housing Commission officer, Neil Riach, and a land agent, Robert Dillon, who was alleged to have paid Riach $31,000. Both were later jailed. Gowans cleared ministers of implication, although he criticised what he said was the slack administration of the housing portfolio. However, there was one Liberal casualty, but at a federal level. Family interests of the then Federal Treasurer, Phillip Lynch, were discovered during the Gowans inquiry to have profited from Melbourne land dealings. Lynch was embarrassed into resigning.

Five months after tabling of the Gowans report, Vance Dickie also resigned, on health grounds, ahead of the 1979 election. During the lead-up to the election, a new Minister for Housing, Geoffrey Hayes, commissioned a new inquiry into further land dealings. When it queried only one transaction, the Hamer Cabinet ruled out any more investigations. The Hamer Government scraped back in, surviving a five per cent swing against it.

Immediately after the election, after Hayes was stripped of his portfolio, and his replacement, Brian Dixon, let slip that he had referred a number of files to the police, claims ensued that the Government had covered them up before the election and thus deceived the voters.

Within a month of the election, the Government was pushed into establishing a Royal Commission. Like the Gowans inquiry, it found no evidence of criminal conduct at ministerial level, but again criticised ministerial oversight of land transactions. Hamer's premiership foundered, and he was dumped, retiring with a knighthood as Sir Rupert Hamer. His replacement, the gentleman politician Lindsay Thompson, soon faced an election.

As statesman in retirement, Sir Henry Bolte mused that the election by then was already lost. 'It was lost for Lindsay Thompson, lost before he got there. Lindsay was Premier for only six months of the Government. He didn't get a go until it was all over bar the shouting.'

4

The Cain Ascendancy

When John Cain led the Labor Party from 27 years in the political wilderness to win power in 1982, nobody was in doubt that he would bring a new order to Victoria. A suburban solicitor, his homely, cautious style endeared him to people in all walks of life. His prudent, if not miserly approach to finances quickly engendered a belief that the State was in good economic hands. His prudish, if not dullish, outlook on lifestyle issues soon earned him his father's mantle of 'Honest John'; indeed, universal acceptance as 'Mr Squeaky Clean', a rare nickname for a politician.

When the report of the inquiry into Labor-controlled Richmond Council, ordered in 1981 by the outgoing Liberal Government, was tabled in Parliament in June 1982, Cain acted decisively, regardless of political affiliation. Alastair Nicholson, QC, produced a damning 900-page report. Cain dismissed the council and installed an administrator, and prosecutions were launched. In one case, Vasilios Sevastropolous was sentenced to imprisonment for more than a year on 32 counts of forging postal ballots.

Similarly, when the report of a Royal Commission into the Builders Labourers' Federation, ordered in 1981 jointly by the outgoing State Liberal Government and the Liberal Federal Government of Malcolm Fraser, was tabled in October 1982, Cain again acted positively. The Royal Commissioner, John Winneke, QC, found evidence of bribery and secret commissions. Subsequently, after a further police investigation into union standover tactics, the Cain administration acted to have the union deregistered.

In the meantime, prosecutions were initiated over secret commissions, leading to the jailing of the union's federal secretary, Norm Gallagher.

In so acting, Cain recalled that he had been accused during the election in 'high places as well as low' of following a line that any prosecutions arising from the Winneke commission would not proceed.

'The Government's duty is clear,' he said. 'The law has to be applied, in respect of all persons regardless of their occupation or their interests or anything else.'

Not surprisingly, a haunting cause célèbre arose over his role at that time in the dropping of charges against three identities involved in a company collapse.

Almost from the time he entered Parliament as a backbencher in 1976, Cain had championed the cause of Victorians who had lost more than $2 million in the North Deborah and Lefroy fraud.

Cain ridiculed the Hamer administration for not pushing ahead with prosecutions.

As Opposition spokesman on legal matters, Cain harried Attorney-General Haddon Storey, who received a secret report on the investigation from barrister Phillip Cummins on 23 April 1978. In a letter to Cain on 8 May 1978, Storey advised that a separate report on criminal proceedings had been delivered by Cummins.

In April 1981, Cain complained in Parliament: '... no action of a specific nature has been taken against any person associated with those companies ... This is a case, on the face of it, of either gross incompetence or a cover-up of some proportions.'

The following month, on 15 May, Cummins wrote a memorandum containing recommendations for prosecutions, largely for company offences. Police were then assigned to pursue the case in support of the corporate affairs inquiry.

In March 1982, three men were arrested and charged with criminal offences: one from Melbourne, Cyril Maskiell, and two from Sydney, Bela Csidei and Malcolm Llewellyn-Dance, all on warrants from the Victorian Government. They were charged with conspiring between 1 January 1972 and 13 June 1972 to defraud shareholders of North Deborah Mining and Industrial Limited, and Lefroy Minerals. On 31 March 1982, barrister Paul Willee, acting as Prosecutor for the Queen, advised the commercial crime group that 'every effort is to be continued to bring these offenders to book in Victoria'. Then an election was held in April – and Cain assumed power. And things changed.

Within months, a memorandum dated 20 August to the Victorian Commissioner for Corporate Affairs, Mrs J. Wade, from the Acting Secretary to the Law Department, noted that in the light of advice from the Solicitor-General (Daryl Dawson, later made a judge of the High Court), 'we should not proceed with any prosecutions'. On the same day, Willee (later chief legal counsel for the National Crime Authority) wrote to solicitors for the defendants advising them that the charges were to be withdrawn. When investigating police heard about it in October, they were told by Willee that John Cain, then Attorney-General as well as Premier, had decided not to proceed. In commending investigators for their work, Willee wrote, 'No doubt it is always galling to find so many months of painstaking work apparently wasted'.

The investigators were not mollified. They were less happy when, on 12 November, Cain issued a public statement boasting that breaches of law uncovered by Victoria's corporate affairs office and other bodies would be pursued by the Victorian Government without fear or favour. Cain was quoted as saying he was determined to see that justice was meted out to all transgressors. In saying so, he signalled a crackdown on white collar crime.

On 21 November, days before the main defendants were due back in court in Sydney on remand for an extradition hearing, an extraordinary meeting was called by the Director of Public Prosecutions, John Phillips (appointed chairman of the National Crime Authority in 1990). It was attended by the three investigators, Frank Della, a corporate affairs investigator; Hans Brocker, Detective Senior Sergeant; and Lorne Campbell, Detective Senior Constable, along with Ken Brown, Superintendent in charge of the Fraud Squad, and Chief Commissioner of Police, Mick Miller.

In a revealing file memo, Campbell recorded his account of that meeting: 'Mr Phillips, referring to written text, gave a lengthy summary of what had gone before in the handling of this matter, going right back to the appointment of Mr Cummins as inspector under the Companies Act. He invited us to stop him if we picked up any inaccuracies. The summary was fairly complete, and as far as I could see, accurate. Mr Phillips also made some brief comments about the law relating to the independence of the police and the relationship between the police and the executive arm of government. He made a rather vague suggestion that it was arguable that the Chief Commissioner was beholden to government direction in the administration of the law. Mr Miller quickly pointed out that this was not the position as he understood it.

'Mr Phillips went on to speak of the police brief prepared by Brocker and myself against Maskiell, Csidei and Llewellyn-Dance. He said he had read the brief and found it to be viable, but went on to say that the matter had gone beyond redemption because a responsible officer of the State of Victoria, under official letterheads, had given a written undertaking to the three accused that proceedings against them would be discontinued, and that in the light of this, if there were fresh charges laid, they would cause the Government a great deal of difficulty and embarrassment. I told Mr Phillips that I was aware of the existence of these letters and had copies of them. I said I was surprised that he should use them as the basis of an argument to let the matters rest because they had no right to exist. … I had never seen them as being a bar to renewed action. Mr Phillips conceded that these letters may not have had a sound legal basis, but because they had an official origin, they still presented a problem. He made the point that he was not expecting us to make up our minds then and there as to our attitude to the matters, but that we were entitled to go away and think about it before giving him an answer. He went on to say that if we chose to issue fresh informations and if the matter resulted in committals for trial, he would have to then exercise his power as DPP to enter a nolle prosequi. Mr Miller then commented that if that was the situation, there didn't seem to be much point in our going away and thinking about it. Senior Sgt Brocker and I agreed and told Mr Phillips that if that was going to be his ultimate attitude, we could tell him on the spot that we would have to let the matter rest. Mr Phillips, in addition to declaring the brief to be viable, had described it as an excellent brief and complimented us on the quality of its preparation.

'Mr Phillips made references to a verbally expressed opinion of Mr Daryl Dawson (as he then was) when as Solicitor-General, he had told Mr Willee that the North Deborah matter was too old to prosecute.

'I had pointed out that this was a case where time had not affected the available evidence, which was almost entirely documentary, and I asked him, since he said he agreed with the sentiment, to explain the rationale behind it. He said that it was an observable fact, being constantly reported to him by his prosecutors, that juries were reluctant to convict on old cases. He said that expense was another important factor. I expressed my disgust at the way this matter was disposed of in a corridor conference. Mr Phillips agreed that it was most unsatisfactory. I made the point that with the abandonment of these prosecutions, the shareholders who had been the victims of the crimes effectively lost all hope of ever getting anything back. Senior Sergeant Brocker and myself expressed our feelings about the U-turn taken in the matter by the Prosecutor, Mr Willee, who previously had expressed great confidence in the brief, but suddenly found it convenient to write the matter off.

'Mr Miller and Mr Brown also commented on the fact that the victims were effectively abandoned and Mr Miller described the handling of the matter by the Law Department, as it then was, as cavalier and laissez-faire.

'Mr Phillips seemed apologetic about the outcome, but made the observation that loyalty required us to take the matter no further.

'The meeting closed at about 4.40 pm, having started late due to Mr Miller being delayed.

'Senior Sergeant Brocker and I discussed the matter later – both quite dissatisfied with the situation and we both feel that the reasons advanced by Mr Phillips were unsatisfactory. We resolved that it was clearly inappropriate in the face of a guaranteed nolle prosequi to reopen the case. We would simply be flushing more public money down the sewer and could well end up being severely criticised for it.'

On 23 November, a telex message signed by the chief of the Victorian CIB, Phil Bennett, was sent to the Sydney fraud squad: 'By direction of the Attorney-General for the State of Victoria [John Cain] the matters relating to Csidei and Llewellyn-Dance are to be withdrawn in Sydney tomorrow. Requesting your assistance.'

Thus, in Sydney's Castlereagh Street Court on 24 November 1982, when the charges were withdrawn, the court was told it was on instructions from the Victorian Government.

In a ministerial statement to Parliament on 1 December, Cain said he had accepted the advice of the Solicitor-General and Crown Counsel in deciding to withdraw the charges. 'No prosecution, or the decision not to prosecute, has been influenced by any political, religious or racial consideration,' said Cain. 'I reject any suggestion to the contrary. It is desirable that these matters should be removed from the political arena.' Cain's action coincided with the withdrawal of a case by the NSW Labor Government of Neville Wran.

Bela Csidei was a key figure in the NSW case, which involved charges of fraud and conspiracy against Alexander and Thomas Barton over two companies, Bounty Oil and Harbourside Oil.

During much-publicised hearings, Barton had alleged that Csidei had been acting in association with Sir Peter Abeles in 1972 when Csidei had bought companies from Barton, including North Deborah and Lefroy. The Crown announced it intended calling Abeles but, on the day he was due to appear, the then NSW Attorney-General, Frank Walker, issued ex officio indictments. Abeles did not appear. Afterwards, the NSW Government rushed through Parliament a controversial Evidence Amendment Act specifically to allow the Government to withhold documents from the Barton case. The legislation was never to be used, since the case never proceeded before a judge and jury.

It was dropped by the Wran administration in August 1982 – the same month Cain decided to also withdraw the Victorian case.

In Sydney, Csidei in particular, was notorious.

In 1978, during a trial that resulted in Csidei being jailed over a marijuana plantation in the Northern Territory, evidence was given that Csidei had borrowed $10,000 from an

American mafia hitman, Jimmy 'The Weasel' Fratianno, and that Fratianno had provided him with marijuana seeds. Csidei also was linked with since jailed San Francisco boss of the notorious Teamsters Union, Rudy Tham.

Several years after the withdrawal of the Victorian charges against him, Csidei was charged with fraud again – this time in Germany, where he was jailed.

A naivety about the real state of organised crime has prompted classic instances of well-meaning Victorians misdirecting attention away from real targets.

It was the same syndrome exemplified by the 1980 report compiled by Victorian Liberal Party backbenchers, promoted as a breakthrough in identifying 'key structures of organised crime in Australia' yet failed to identify anybody actually involved in organised crime in Victoria.

Organised crime is a fact of life in all world cities the size of Melbourne. It is a universal axiom that its extent is governed by patronage and protection. In that respect, Melbourne has been better off than many places. Which may explain why Melbourne media devotes more space to exposing Sydney's mores than it does to Melbourne's sores in its own backyard.

As Dr James Jupp, former lecturer in political science at Melbourne University, commented in 1986 in a chapter entitled 'Political Culture' in *The Sydney-Melbourne Book*, 'Corruption and organised crime are frowned upon and only tolerated if they maintain a low profile or form part of the honours system or normal course of business.' What goes on in Sydney does go on in Melbourne. Except that Melbourne in modern times has tended to do more about it.

Notwithstanding a long history of police and political corruption, Melbourne in modern times at least has been relatively free of institutionalised corruption that has facilitated the growth of syndicated crime in Sydney over the past two decades. Whereas NSW has steadfastly resisted perennial demands for any full-scale inquiry into police activities, the Victorian police force has been purged by a number of wide-ranging inquiries.

During the latter period of the Sir Rupert Hamer period, the short term of Lindsay Thompson, and under John Cain, Victorians became less tolerant of corruption, either in their police force or politics. In the absence of the police and political protection that encouraged a relatively well ordered system for the underworld rackets in Sydney, the underworld in Melbourne, however, has been very much akin to the law of the jungle.

One of the reasons advanced for the greater tendency for violence among Melbourne criminals underlines the essential difference between Sydney and Melbourne; with less opportunity to achieve power through corruption, Melbourne criminals resort to bullets instead of bribes.

Invariably, whenever feuds have broken out in Sydney, entrenched interests more used to settled times through corruption have brought in hit-men from Melbourne to do the dirty work. Such was the case with Chris Flannery, known as 'Rent-a-Kill', who made his name in Melbourne before being hired at the outbreak of gang warfare in the early 1980s resulting in eight deaths. Flannery, accused of carrying out some of them on contract, himself disappeared, reportedly disposed of by Sydney gangster George Freeman as part of the terms of an eventual peace treaty in May 1985.

In the illegal gambling field, the traditional money pot for organised crime, Melbourne has never been as wide open as Sydney. Nonetheless, an exposé in November 1987 by *Age* 'Insight' disclosed that police had identified an astonishing 700 establishments in Melbourne and key country centres that had been used for illegal gambling. These, of course, included ethnic card games. Maybe because of its more upfront, larger casinos, Sydney and its environs, including Newcastle and Wollongong, have never boasted more than 350. Insight was able to emphasis that most in Victoria had been raided, though major establishments such as the Zorro Club in Acland Street, St Kilda, continued to flourish. Otherwise known as Charlie's Place, after its operator Charlie Wootton, the Zorro Club operated virtually uninterrupted for nearly two decades, outlasting even Sydney's most notorious, such as the Forbes, Goulburn and Kellet Clubs, or protected casinos in Brisbane exposed by the Fitzgerald inquiry.

While turnover for SP rackets in NSW has been put at $1800 million a year, the figure for Victoria, according to an estimate from one judicial inquiry, would be around $1000 million. Separate inquiries set up under the Cain Government resulted in Victoria continuing to outlaw poker machines and legal casinos for fear of infiltration by organised crime. Cain also banned pornography, which had flourished under the Liberals.

Curiously, however, the Cain Government legalised brothels in 1985, ostensibly to stop organised crime and police corruption in the vice field.

Melbourne had long had the distinction of being Australia's brothel capital. A parliamentary inquiry in NSW found that NSW had 2200 prostitutes.

A Government inquiry in Victoria found that Victoria had between 3000 and 4000. Legalisation has conferred legitimacy and fortune on operators such as John Trimbole, nephew of deceased drug boss Bob Trimbole. Through legalisation, John Trimbole's brothel, The Daily Planet, Melbourne's biggest, was able to be advertised for sale at more than $12 million.

In the lead up to legalisation in 1985, Victoria's minister in charge of brothels, Evan Walker, wrote to all known brothel owners a number of times, encouraging them to apply for permits so that they could be licensed. Addressing them as 'Dear Occupier', Walker wrote in one letter on 3 April 1985: '... The Government realises there have been some difficulties experienced by the industry in finding appropriate sites for which to make applications for brothels, but it is still somewhat surprised at the small number of applications made, compared with the total number of brothels existing ... I emphasise that if you intend to remain in the industry, it is in your interest to apply for a planning permit, and I urge your consideration of this letter.' Walker later circularised each and every one of the State's cities, towns and shires with specific directions that none could any longer ban brothels from their area.

In the illicit drug trade at least, Melbourne is said to have fewer heroin addicts than Sydney. But it does have a more entrenched trade in amphetamines, controlled by bikie gang members. And, with cocaine becoming more fashionable, it has emerged as a cocaine capital. Lawyers as well as police have been caught out for involvement in the drug trade. Many drug syndicates have been found to have links with Sydney.

Everybody in Sydney, if not throughout Australia, knew of Sydney crime boss George Freeman, usually referred to as 'a colourful racing identity'. Relatively few people in Melbourne, and less so elsewhere, know of Charlie Wootton, seldom referred to at all.

In November 1988, when Victorian police, in a commando-style raid, swung down from the top of a 15-storey building on ropes and smashed through windows of an upstairs gambling joint to arrest Wootton and others, not one word appeared in the Melbourne press. Such is the difference between Melbourne and Sydney.

Freeman, who died in 1990, was always in the news. He

even published his own autobiography, bragging about his involvement in various activities, including how he masterminded the changeover from old-style, backstreet baccarat to modern, shopfront casinos. Wootton has rarely been publicised. He has never talked, let alone entertained writing a book about how he has managed to operate for so long when his name has become synonymous in Melbourne's underworld with illegal gambling. Indeed, Wootton epitomises the differences – and similarities – between Sydney and Melbourne. Sydney is brash, upfront. Whereas Melbourne is conservative, subtle.

George Freeman has always been George Freeman, and let everybody know it, driving a Mercedes with personalised GF number plates. On many occasions, he invited the media to profile his Dallas-style mansion at Yowie Bay.

Charlie Wootton has played it low-key, using aliases, Charles Nugent or Ronald Hope, preferring to be chauffeured in a Rolls-Royce. He once punched a man who dared call on him at his Victorian-style mansion in Brighton's Golden Mile.

Wootton received only brief attention from the Royal Commission into the Federated Ship Painters and Dockers' Union conducted by Mr Frank Costigan, QC, though he was linked with Freeman. Freeman was described as being 'heavily involved in illegal gambling (in Sydney)' and Wootton as being 'the leading figure in the control of illegal gambling (in Melbourne)'.

In evidence, Billy 'The Texan' Longley described Wootton as one of the 'faceless men behind the docks' who got a 'cut from the wharves' and was a 'multi-millionaire' with investments in baccarat, trotting and drugs. Wootton displays his painter and docker union membership certificate in his office at St Kilda. The only time there is any certainty that his name will be found in newspapers is when such identities place bereavement notices in Melbourne's mass circulation *Herald-Sun*, a traditional Victorian nicety whenever there is an underworld death.

In a report by a joint Commonwealth–NSW task force on drugs, tabled in Federal Parliament in 1983, Wootton was described as a Melbourne criminal and linked to ex-NSW policeman and drug trafficker, Murray Riley. Like Freeman, Riley's exploits have been well chronicled. He was linked with the same America mafia identities as was Bela Csidei. Not so Wootton.

A belated profile was pieced together by Insight in the *Age* in November 1987 under the byline of Paul Robinson, which traced his 'chequered career' since leaving school at 15 to work on the waterfront. In 1958, at age 17, Wootton was present when Melbourne's standover king of the 1940s and 1950s, Freddy 'The Frog' Harrison, was executed in full view of dozens of people during a pay parade at 13 South Wharf. Wootton was stopped by a policeman in a street nearby, while carrying a box of shells. Wootton failed to appear when called as a witness at the inquest.

One of Australia's most publicised drug busts followed a legal telephone tap that recorded a painter and docker, Stephen Nittes, contacting Charlie Wootton about acting as a distributor in Melbourne for part of a $40 million shipment of cannabis imported from Lebanon by a Sydney syndicate including a friend of George Freeman's, Nicholas Paltos, a doctor; Graham 'Croc' Palmer, a casino operator; and Ross Karp, a solicitor. On 4 December 1984, after Karp met Nittes under police surveillance at Fawkner Park, South Yarra, they left in different directions, then Karp re-entered the park, and this time met Wootton. Nittes was later recorded telling an associate, 'if you ever get into trouble with the police, ring up Charlie Wootton'.

With the establishment of a National Crime Authority in

July 1984, the real, hidden extent of organised crime in Melbourne came under scrutiny. Dozens of identities have been put before the courts, among them some whose tentacles had spread not only interstate but overseas.

Under a reference code-named Freeboot, using Royal Commission-type powers, the NCA concentrated on targets that had been overlooked or proved beyond the resources of the normal arms of the law. Under the chairmanship of a Sydney judge, Don Stewart, and authority members, Max Bingham (later foundation chairman of the Queensland Criminal Justice Commission) and independent-minded Melbourne barrister Peter Clark, the NCA in Melbourne enjoyed considerable success, within limitations imposed under the NCA Act.

In 1989, when Stewart retired, it had been expected that Clark would have been appointed chairman. Instead, Clark was excluded in favour of another Melbourne barrister, Peter Faris, who lasted but eight months, resigning suddenly, during a health breakdown, after it was publicly disclosed that he had been stopped by police outside a Melbourne brothel.

In 1990, Faris was replaced by another Victorian, John Phillips, former Victorian Director of Public Prosecutions then a judge of the Supreme Court of Victoria. Justice Phillips announced at the outset that he intended to change the focus of the NCA to white collar crime, a break from the racket-busting pattern set by Justice Stewart. A popular approach in Victoria (even though under Stewart more than 50 per cent of NCA resources in Melbourne already, in fact, had been devoted to white collar fraud), the Phillips switch did not go down all that well in Sydney, where a series of citizen committees had risked much in campaigning for years to get an NCA to target the Mr Bigs of organised crime.

Once public concern over what should be done about organised crime evolved into a national issue rather than simply a NSW problem, Victorian Government and legal interests hijacked the debate.

During Cain's first year in office, Liberal Prime Minister Malcolm Fraser put through legislation for establishment of a National Crimes Commission. Cain opposed it. Unfortunately, Fraser overlooked to proclaim the legislation before hurrying into an election early in 1983, when he was ousted by the Labor Party's Bob Hawke. The legislation lapsed.

In July 1983, the Hawke Government hosted a national summit in Parliament House, Canberra, to consider what should be done. Royal Commissioners and others spoke in support of the Fraser model for a standing commission with power to hold Royal Commission-style public hearings. Opposition was spearheaded by the Victorian Government, with Cain's legal adviser, Howard Nathan (later made a judge of the Supreme Court of Victoria) pressing for a coordinated intelligence gathering secretariat or authority only, with ad hoc Royal Commissions only where deemed necessary. There was considerable disagreement, even among Victorian representatives, with Kim Beazley, Acting Special Minister of State, saying that summit participants were 'privileged to witness in public what is generally conducted in private – the deliberations of the Victorian Bar Council'. In fact, the outcome of the summit was deliberated in private, with Victoria coming out on top. Within a week, a working party met in Nathan's office in Melbourne and reached consensus on what was to become the National Crime Authority, embodying secrecy provisions to restrict public hearings.

In February 1991, Justice Phillips publicly called for amendments to the secrecy provisions, to allow public hearings. As observed by Jo Chandler in the *Age*, 'It would be mischievous to abuse the facility of hindsight – to say nothing of the analogy – and mention the baby who went out with the bath water. But it is appropriate to note that chairman Phillips' self-declared mission to reform the NCA has taken the authority right back to basics.'

As other events were to prove, a misplaced holier-than-thou attitude was to cost Victoria dearly in the wash up of the Cain era.

5
Stinky Limits

A stink over a 'Mr Stinky' in 1985 exposed Victoria's conspicuous tradition of allowing more rights for criminals than for victims of crime. Its police force, compared with others around Australia, has always been the one with the least powers to do its job. Throughout the terms of successive governments of all political persuasions, the force has been denied the right to demand fingerprints and photographs of suspects, demand names and addresses, require suspects to take part in identity parades – or even search a suspect. The imbalance was brought home to the Cain administration by the much-publicised case of Raymond 'Mr Stinky' Edmunds, murderer and rapist.

In 1966, Edmunds was suspected for the double murder of two teenagers, Abina Madill and Garry Heywood, in the Victorian country town of Shepparton. Abina had been raped. Edmunds again was suspected of two further murders, as well as more than 32 sexual attacks on women. Significantly, Edmunds had in fact been arrested previously, on a minor matter, in the 1950s. But Victorian law precluded mandatory fingerprinting. If Edmunds had been fingerprinted then, his prints would have matched prints taken from the 1966 murder scene – and the case would have been solved. Edmunds was able therefore to continue his violent rampage throughout nearly two decades. Finally, Edmunds was positively linked to the Shepparton murder and subsequent sex crimes only after being arrested by NSW police for exposing himself in public across the border from Victoria in Albury in 1985. He was then fingerprinted – and so only by a chance matching up of the fingerprints was it suddenly proved that he was guilty of the murders and rapes.

Even so, Victorian police remain limited. After police did arrest Edmunds, they had to comply with an interviewing deadline. Under Section 460 of the Victorian Crimes Act, police were confined to only six hours in which to question a suspect. Once the time limit expired, any offender had to be taken before a court where he had to agree to a further session with police or the questioning was over. Edmunds did agree to two extensions. Nonetheless, because of the deadlines, time ran out for questioning Edmunds over all offences of which he was suspected. Thus he was never charged over the majority of offences police were convinced he committed. He was convicted and jailed over the Shepparton murders.

But police claimed he was suspected also of the murder of another teenage girl, Anne Richardson, aged 16, who was abducted from the main street of Albury in October 1973. Her body was found in the Murray River. Police also wanted to question him about the murder of Elaine Jones, a housewife whose body also was found in the Murray River. Her husband died of a heart attack while trying to retrieve her body from the river.

The scandal of the Mr Stinky case was graphically illustrated in a book titled *Cuckoo* by journalist Andrew Rule. In a foreword, retiring Chief Commissioner of Police, Mick Miller, wrote, '... had Edmunds committed the same offence south of the Murray River instead of in Albury – only a few kilometres away – he could have refused to be routinely fingerprinted. The case, rightly, became a cause célèbre for police, victims and others who believed Victoria's fingerprint laws were out of step with other States, other countries and common sense.'

Under pressure, the Cain Government abandoned the six-hour questioning limit for police, but allowed them limited power to fingerprint – if they could convince a court that they had evidence pointing to the suspect and needed prints as part of the investigation. Victoria remained the only State prohibiting police from obliging a suspect to take part in an identity parade.

It continued to share with Western Australia the dubious distinction of not allowing the power to photograph suspects. Victorian police still cannot demand names and addresses, unless for traffic offences, to collect Government revenue. On an experimental basis only, from June 1990, police were extended limited power, but on a court order, to force a blood sample from a suspect to compare with forensic evidence gathered in murder and sex cases.

In public outbursts, police have continually voiced concern over what they see as ingrained tendencies of the Victorian criminal justice system to slant towards the accused at the expense of victims. Routinely, at least five of those on the top 10 most wanted list of criminals in Victoria have been criminals already caught and charged with serious offences, including international drug trafficking, only to be granted bail.

The relationship between senior police and politicians in Victoria has always been fragile. A convention, based on the British criminal justice system, has meant that police are given some autonomy on operational matters. Unlike all other public servants, police are not held directly subordinate to the political leaders on a day-to-day basis. The convention is that police should be subordinate to the law and should be seen to be separate from the government of the day – not to be hired 'muscle' for the politicians.

In some Australian States, police forces have been less than independent from their governments. In Queensland for example, in 1983, the now disgraced Commissioner, Terry Lewis, gave a poorly-disguised election speech for Bjelke-Petersen's National Party. Lewis was later knighted. In Victoria, senior police have been able to make public comments that have been severely critical of government policy.

Time after time police have gone over the top of their political 'masters' to appeal to the public on certain issues. Imagine the permanent public service head of the Health or Education Departments slagging off at the government over policy or budget? It just does not happen. Public servants are supposed to shut up and carry out government policy. But the police in Victoria have developed their own voice. They are the only government department that has its own media liaison machine, separate to government control.

In years gone by, it did not really matter that much. Senior police tended to be slightly to the right of Genghis Khan on the political spectrum, and would call for certain police powers that would never be granted in a democracy. They failed to become involved in the serious debate on law and order by talking of castrating rapists, bringing back conscription to return discipline to society, and other sundry matters that were only diversions. When Mick Miller became Chief Commissioner in 1977, he brought with him a form of thoughtful articulateness that made people listen. Miller was prepared to stimulate public debate on many areas within the criminal justice system.

Over his more than 10 years as Chief Commissioner, he questioned the role of juries, called for at least another 2000 police, queried the accused's right to an unsworn statement from the dock and championed the rights of victims of crimes. Many of his senior officers started to do the same. No longer were senior police seen as staid, somewhat wooden men, unlikely to generate gems of original thought.

Miller's men changed the direction. Not only did they speak openly and forcefully about what they wanted – people began to listen.

The drug problem began to hit home, crime rates continued to rise and burglary rates were out of control.

In late 1987 the Cain Government conducted confidential polls to see what would be likely to be serious election issues. They found that law and order was in the top three concerns for people interviewed.

The Opposition had made it clear that they were going to push the law and order issue as a major plank in their election campaign. Late in 1987 the Government moved its number one troubleshooter, Steve Crabb, into the police and prisons portfolios. Crabb, a Scottish immigrant with a canny grasp of the pragmatic, had the reputation as a man who could handle political hot spots. Crabb was considered a politician who got things done, but not one with a great eye for detail. His brief was obvious: make sure that law and order would not damage the Government in an election that would soon be due.

One of the first things Crabb did was to hire a new 'mouthpiece', a spokesman and damage control expert to deal with the media. He lured Jim Tennison, veteran chief police reporter of the *Sun*, to fill the role.

One of the reasons that police issues always tend to be of concern to governments was that there was a large contingent of journalists from the main media outlets who report exclusively on police matters. These journalists work with police, drink with them, work in the building next to the CIB headquarters, and tend to mirror police concerns. Most journalists who deal on State political matters work in close proximity to the politicians. The political journalists and the politicians develop working relationships that tend to be mutually beneficial. In just the same way the police reporters and the police develop strong ties. By getting Tennison, Crabb was able to 'tap in' to the group of journalists who were the ones who consistently wrote the stories on police powers. It was just one part of a campaign of damage control.

Under Crabb, the Government seemed more sympathetic to police requests, including finding nearly $4 million more for the police in early 1988 on top of its normal budget allocation.

He also found money for new equipment and started to update many antiquated police stations. He introduced limited access to phone tapping and oversaw the compulsory audio taping of suspects being interviewed over indictable offences. Whatever the reason for the Government's seemingly temporary pro-police line, it appeared to take the heat out of the law and order issue. The Government was returned to power in October 1988.

In April 1990, Crabb was moved from the police portfolio. Government polls then showed that the law and order issue was nowhere near as potent as it had been a few years earlier. From the middle of 1989 until early 1990 confidential Government polls showed that law and order was off the agenda as a major political issue to voters.

The police ministerial baton was passed to Mal Sandon, a novice minister.

The crime rate in Victoria has more than doubled in 10 years, according to former deputy commissioner Paul Delianis. He said that senior police had been forced to reduce services because of lack of funds. Delianis said that up until 1984 fully-trained detectives investigated all house burglaries. Now only burglaries where more than $500 worth of property was stolen were fully investigated because of a lack of detectives.

The role of policing has changed and enlarged in the past decade. Areas such as community policing, task forcing, transit duties and drug detection have proved draining on police resources.

Miller's successor as Chief Commissioner, Kel Glare, has said that reductions in budget were causing grave damage. He told the *Sunday Age* that many police were exhausted and demoralised by working long hours. 'We have been starved for resources as a police force for the last 40 years,' he said. Opposition criticism over police powers and resources has always sounded hollow. When the Liberal Party was in government for 27 years, it provided only the bare minimum for the force.

Also, it did not extend police powers and some Liberal police ministers did not devote a great deal of time to the portfolio.

The police role has had to expand as society has become more violent. In 1983 the police nerve centre, D24, received 262,102 calls. In 1988-89 the number was 706,169 calls. Between 1987-88 and 1988-89 the number of jobs despatched to police units increased by more than 26,000 from 422,353 to 448,388. The major crime index also showed the massive increase in police work. In 1945, major crime offences detected were 21,483. In 1988-89 it was 314,755.

Studies on police response times showed that citizens could get a prostitute or a pizza delivered to their homes quicker than they could get a policeman. The average response time for police to attend was 32 minutes. Escort services and pizza parlours boasted home calls within 30 minutes.

The police force has been further destabilised by a new superannuation scheme that enables police to retire at a far earlier age. The system, known as the Emergency Services Superannuation Scheme, was brought in at the beginning of 1987. It was designed on the basis that police, firefighters and ambulance officers deserve to able to retire earlier. One of the immediate effects of the scheme was that the police force lost between 700 and 800 members per year, many of them opting to leave when in the prime of their careers, when they were aged in their 30s and 40s. The force lost many key people. After ESSS, the average age of the force dropped to about 32 years, with 10 years' experience in the job. Only two per cent of the force was over 50 years, compared with 10 per cent for the general Australian work force.

A real running sore in the the criminal justice system has been Victoria's antiquated prison system. For years there has been a political cliche, 'There are no votes in prisons' and the area has been given the bare minimum attention. That all changed after 29 October 1987, when five of Australia's most violent men barricaded themselves into their unit in the top security Jika Jika wing at Pentridge, started a protest fire, and died from the fumes. Murderers Robert Wright, Richard John Morris, David McGauley, and armed robbers James Loughnan and Arthur Gallagher died in the fire.

An inquest conducted by State Coroner Hal Hallenstein turned into a mini judicial inquiry. His report, released on 28 July 1989 after a $1.5 million hearing, slated the Office of Corrections. He found that the department had contributed to the death of the prisoners. Hallenstein said the department had behaved in a way that could be considered corrupt during the inquest, had tried to manipulate evidence and avoid public accountability. Response of staff to the fatal fire had been inept. Hallenstein called on the Government to announce 'an independent and general inquiry into the Office of Corrections and the administration of the prison system in Victoria'.

The Government responded with several separate inquiries, all falling short of the one recommended. One report completed by a police task force headed by Chief Inspector Terry Mulgrew claimed that senior Office of Corrections officers tolerated drug use by inmates in jails. It found that a prisoner and two prison officers formed a private company in questionable circumstances. A female prison officer was living in a de facto relationship with a former inmate, suspected by police of being an active criminal. It was also found that 156 prison officers, almost one in 10, had prior convictions, half which were considered 'of serious concern'. The report also said that some senior prison officers broke the law by not reporting drug offences to police.

Another inquiry in the Hallenstein allegations was headed by a retired Supreme Court judge, Tony Murray, QC. He came down against the Coroner's use of the word 'corrupt' in describing the Office of Corrections. But he found that some individual prison officers lied while giving evidence to the inquest. He also found that the Office of Corrections 'went too far' in trying to paint a favourable picture for the Coroner, but said the department did not organise a cover-up. Another police investigation, by Chief Inspector Graeme McDonald and Senior Sergeant Noel Ashby, into allegations of corruption made by an inmate, found that faction fighting among jail staff was rife. The police could not substantiate allegations made by the inmate, but found that one prison officer could have attempted to intimidate a prisoner to stop him giving evidence in a criminal trial.

The Cain Government inherited a system that was a disaster. It spent more than $200 million on redeveloping prisons and building four new jails since 1982. Before that only one new jail had been built in 100 years. An internal prison service study in late 1989 estimated that Victorian inmates spent $5 million on drugs every year. A national investigation by the Australian Bureau of Criminal Intelligence, under the code-name Alabama, found that some prisoners maintained outside bank accounts to keep money for buying and selling drugs inside jail. The ABCI investigation also found a network of prisoners around Australia who were helped by sympathisers on the outside. It found that prisoners who escaped could be moved from State to State and eventually overseas by the group. According to the ABCI, several safe houses for escapees have been set up in Victoria.

6
Legalised Vice

When Victorian police and Immigration Department officers raided Lady Madison's, a Port Melbourne brothel, in July 1988, it removed any doubt that there were serious problems with legalised brothels. Six Thai women working as prostitutes were taken away and later deported. Each woman was with a client when police arrived late on a Thursday night, and the lobby was crowded with customers. In the 45 minutes police spent at the brothel, another 20 customers arrived.

The six Thai women were happy to be taken away in the raid. One had been forced to work despite having a torn vagina, damaged a few days earlier by a violent customer – she had been given no treatment for the injury. Like her five colleagues, brought out from Thailand on the promise that they could stay in Australia, she was told that she owed $12,000 to the organisation that arranged her travel and that she had to work off the debt. From the thousands of dollars paid by customers (at an average of $50 for half an hour), the women were given $45 a week to buy cosmetics or clothes. Their tourist visas had either expired, or else the condition that prohibits working had been breached.

The women were like hundreds of other Thai prostitutes in Australia; cheap labour making small fortunes for brothel owners and those who 'sell' them – usually in groups of six – to brothels around Australia. According to Noi Apisuk, a representative of a Thai bar workers' and prostitutes' group, Empower, more than 400 Thai women had been lured to

Australia by mid-1988 to work as prostitutes by a group simply known as 'The Triad'.

But the use of illegal immigrants as prostitutes, even in Melbourne's legal brothels, is no offence. Lady Madison's, like more than 60 other buildings in Melbourne, holds a permit to run a legal brothel. At the time of the raid, the building was owned by a company called Pivil Eight Nominees Pty Ltd. The sole shareholder and director was Richard Coombes, a former Victorian policeman who left the force in April 1963.

Like Fred Lelah, a brothel owner who has been convicted of offering a bribe to police and faced other charges, there is no disincentive to use Asian prostitutes. Six illegal Asian immigrants working as prostitutes were taken from Lelah's brothel soon after the Lady Madison's raid.

Australia is a big outlet in the lucrative market of exporting Asian prostitutes to Western countries, and women have been seized in most capital cities. Immigration Department inquiries have led to the sacking of Australian embassy staff overseas for their apparent involvement in 'visa for sale' rackets. In one case, several workers were sacked from the Kuala Lumpur embassy in Malaysia after 75 visas were issued to women with a 'prostitution profile'. Police have received reports that the Japanese crime group the Yakuza is planning to send prostitutes to Australia to service Japanese visitors.

This is no surprise considering Melbourne is regarded as the new frontier for Japanese sex tourists. According to the *Age* correspondent in Tokyo, Tom Ormonde, a national magazine pitched at young businessmen glowingly reviewed a Melbourne brothel in mid-1990, describing the prices as bargains and saying that health screening 'in the Government-sanctioned brothels means you don't have to worry about AIDS'. But the fact that legal brothels in Melbourne, which were made lawful partly to keep criminals out of the industry, can use Asian prostitutes as slaves and not affect their legal status is an indictment on legislation that, in almost all of its well-meant aims, has failed.

The modern history of Melbourne's brothels is one of violence, drugs and police corruption. In the early 1970s, illegal brothels suddenly flourished under the guise of massage parlours and health studios. What caused the sudden upsurge in sex outlets is hard to understand. Perhaps it was identified as an easy way to make money, because those who policed the area were toothless; perhaps street prostitutes and those who worked from home were attracted by the security offered by massage parlours.

Whatever the reason, parlours thrived. Permits for massage parlours were the domain of local councils, which found that if they refused to grant a permit, operators opened up regardless. Court action to close a parlour took about nine months and the maximum fine was $200. Most councils that tried to close a parlour saw it shut down shortly before a court case began, then reopen several doors away. A new assault on the parlour, requiring fresh action, again took months to get to court. By 1975, most councils gave up attempts at closing parlours and instead appealed to the Hamer Liberal Government for tough, new legislation. The Government passed regulations banning the establishment of new massage parlours in residential areas, but the effect was negligible. Parlour owners and councils continued to play the same game through the courts. The rules were still the same, irrespective of whether the parlour was in a 'residential' zone.

By early 1976, police claimed there were 160 massage parlours in metropolitan Melbourne, with 'new parlours cropping up every day'. Melbourne, said one officer, 'has more parlours than any other city in the western world ... it is escalating like a bushfire out of control'. Both statements were most likely exaggerations, but more parlours were opening than closing. Police complained that they could close gaming houses through Supreme Court action, but could not close massage parlours. The upsurge in the parlour industry coincided with the arrival of large quantities of heroin in Australia. According to parlour operators, many prostitutes had smoked marijuana or taken various pills such as Mandrax before heroin arrived; the new drug was more addictive, and proved lucrative for parlour operators who, by supplying workers with the drug, could take their percentage from clients' payments and effectively recover the prostitute's cut as well. And with more money around there came the inevitable violence.

A series of bashings and rapes in 1976 were blamed on Sydney criminals attempting to force their way into the Melbourne vice scene. The year 1977 began with deliberate fires set at three St Kilda Road parlours, the bashing of a brothel owner and the firebombing of a Lamborghini Urraco sports car owned by a man who later became known as the king of Melbourne's massage parlours. Soon afterwards, James Joseph Patrick Kelly was shot and killed as he stood in the doorway of his home in Mary Street, Kew. Kelly operated the exclusive Gentle Touch parlour in St Kilda Road. He was hit in the face and chest by four bullets fired from a .38 pistol. Kelly's killer was never found.

Throughout 1977 and 1978 there was sporadic violence. South Melbourne Council counted 60 massage parlours in a block between Queens Road and St Kilda Road – not one had a permit.

Local councils began calling on the State Government to reform and tighten massage parlour legislation. Police complained that senior officers had ordered them to stay out of parlours because, as the legislation stood, police were only allowed into massage parlours if they were 'invited in'. The Hamer administration began an inquiry into the legislation and, in November 1978, announced a series of changes, partly designed to clear massage parlours from residential areas by increasing fines. Fines for streetwalking prostitutes were boosted. The net effect was that more prostitutes sought work in parlours. Despite the political rhetoric of the day – 'Massage parlours are now in jeopardy' – little changed. Parlours began using legal means to stall any decision, and appealed to higher planning authorities against council decisions. When the avenues of appeal began to run out, they closed down and moved, to begin the process again. Some councils complained that this legal delaying tactic was allowing parlours to stay open for a further 18 months.

In Fitzroy in May and June of 1979, there was a string of fires, shots fired through parlour windows and a prostitute was shot dead. Police investigated the deaths of six prostitutes who died in suspicious circumstances. Although inquests recorded open findings, police suspected the women had deliberately been given fatal overdoses, or 'hot shots'. Rival brothel operators employed strongmen and bashings were common. More subtle messages were conveyed with funeral cars and coffins arriving at the homes of vice identities. In April 1980, Michael James John Erbert, 31, who had been running three massage parlours, was shot four times as he left one of his parlours in Rathdowne Street, Carlton. Erbert died only three months after being released from jail after serving almost four years for manslaughter.

About the same time, the Liberal Cabinet considered a proposal to legalise prostitution, a move supported by the party's State council and a key minister, Brian Dixon. The move was rejected. Instead, the Government moved to raise fines and toughen penalties for prostitution.

In 1982, after the Cain Labor Government was elected, it

decided to implement a policy of legalisation adopted by the Labor Party in 1978. The Government decided to tackle the problem by first setting up an advisory committee.

The committee's report was made public in November 1983 and recommended the decriminalisation of prostitution in legal, controlled brothels. Four months later, the Minister for Planning, Evan Walker, announced that prostitution would be legal. Trade had to be conducted inside premises that had a planning permit. The Government's attitude was that prostitution was a planning problem. On 22 May 1984, as part of the Town and Country Planning Act and the Planning Act, prostitution in brothels with a permit became legal. Walker said that to allow existing parlours to apply for a permit, there would be a 12-month moratorium on the prosecution of brothels. For some owners this was terrific news. It meant no police raids or harassment for 12 months. If they knew they would not get a permit, it was a deadline on making money and getting out.

One parlour owner who took advantage of the moratorium was a quiet, studious man named Ian Dauer. Dauer, chubby and fat-faced, had a remarkable and unusual background – he was a policeman. Dauer's involvement was the clearest example of police corruption in the sex industry in the 1980s – although he certainly wasn't the only bent cop involved. Dauer, a fraud squad detective, began a relationship with a prostitute and, through her, met the owner of the brothel where she worked. Dauer told the owner that he, like other police, wanted to become involved in brothels before they were legalised. The owner later claimed that Dauer said he would arrange police protection for the brothels. A deal was struck and, within a week, Dauer came up with $20,000 in cash, about the equivalent of his annual after-tax salary, for a half-share in one of the owner's brothels. Dauer came unstuck when one of his employees was arrested by police. In a bid to get himself off the impending charges, the employee volunteered that he knew of a policeman working in the trade.

From there a vice squad inquiry intensified, but within a week word got back to Dauer, presumably from information leaked by police colleagues. Dauer, with four other men, kidnapped the employee and bashed him, threatening him with death. The bashing was Dauer's undoing: he was later arrested, convicted of assault and kidnapping, sacked from the force and sentenced to a minimum of six years in jail.

Soon after the 12-month brothel moratorium began, the Victorian Government commissioned Marcia Neave, a professor of law at Melbourne University, to study the prostitution industry and come up with solutions that would be the framework for legislation. All but one of her 90 recommendations – to set up red light districts – were accepted. Laws were drafted and in 1986 they were put to Parliament. Before this happened, the legalisation ball was well and truly rolling. When the moratorium had ended in mid-1985, some 12 months before the legislation went before Parliament, about 20 brothels had been granted permits under planning laws, and many others were awaiting decisions on their applications. At the time, Evan Walker, as 'minister in charge of brothels', said in a press release: 'Brothels are now regulated to a degree which should eliminate many complaints and remove criminals and children from their operations.' Despite the Government's bravado, it was clear that the planning laws were flawed and better laws were needed.

Under the planning guidelines, permit holders were restricted from having interests in more than one brothel, and it was illegal for people convicted of an indictable offence or a drug offence in the preceding five years to hold a permit. But a criminal could own the land and lease the brothel to someone without a criminal record, put up a 'front man' or, more conveniently, hide the ownership through company structures. And the legislation merely required that the permit holder not be a recently-convicted criminal. Someone released from jail after serving six years for rape and manslaughter could apply for a permit without being exempt.

Neave recognised these problems and proposed solutions: she had a grand plan. Neave wanted the vice industry to be competitive, allowing small and big business to compete in the market. She proposed that big businesses, brothels with three or more women, would need a permit to operate. Two prostitutes would need a planning permit – similar to a permit that an all-night convenience store would require – and a solo prostitute working from home would need no form of regulation. To do this, all criminal sanctions relating to prostitution needed to be removed. While selling one's body for sex is not an offence, soliciting for prostitution, using a premises for habitual prostitution and living off the earnings were all illegal. Neave considered these laws outdated and unnecessary. If, for example, the laws were repealed and a street prostitute made a nuisance of herself, the prostitute could still be charged with offensive behaviour or other 'street' offences. There were fall back positions.

The Government now needed to pass the laws to make legalised brothels work – to keep out criminals and prevent exploitation of women and children. But there was one big problem: the Opposition parties controlled the upper house and so had the final say on what could become law.

They were split into two camps: the National Party, whose members wanted to block the legislation at any cost because it 'would lower moral standards', and the Liberals, who saw serious drawbacks in the proposals.

The Liberals were the key to the passing of the legislation. If they blocked anything, they would have National support and the proposal would fail. If they agreed with the legislation, they could vote with the Government and easily outnumber the Nationals.

The Liberals had numerous concerns about the legislation, the biggest stemming from police briefings that big brothel owners were leasing rows of houses, and planned to install solo prostitutes to get around the licensing provisions. It was a huge loophole that the Liberals would not allow to pass. Their solution was that all prostitutes would require permits, and they made another 50 or so changes to the legislation before it was put to the vote. The Nationals voted against; the Liberals and Labor Party voted for the new laws and they were passed, but the Government was far from happy. The modified legislation remained dormant for six months. At various times the Government threatened to abandon proclaiming the laws and any plans to reform prostitution. In July 1987, the Government decided to make only half the legislation law. The sections dealing with licensing were ditched, with the Government itself conceding it was a 'lame duck' result. By this time there were 47 legal brothels.

According to the Prostitutes Collective of Victoria, Melbourne had about 4000 prostitutes. Of those, 900 worked in brothels, around 40 on St Kilda's streets, and the rest in escort agencies (the number, they said, was anyone's guess) and in 'cottage industries' – women who worked from home and saw a handful of clients each week. The collective said street workers used to number around 150, but had decreased primarily because of increased police 'harassment'. Because of the legislation, street workers became the visible law-breakers, so were frequently arrested. Many later moved into legal brothels or into the escort business, where all that is needed is an advertisement and a telephone number; it may still be illegal, but there is less chance of attracting police attention.

The escort agency business also increased because women found it easier than working for those owning brothels. Two or three women may buy an answering machine and put an advertisement in *Truth*. In that way they don't lose the commission they would have to pay a brothel owner (often around 50 per cent). They also avoid other problems: paying for a taxi to get to work (most brothels are in industrial areas because they are banned from residential areas by law), and 'fines' imposed by brothel owners over issues such as make-up or clothing, and more serious problems.

Many women have also been 'taxed' by their employers, but at the end of the financial year have been denied group certificates. The result is that many who worked in illegal brothels and on the street have moved 'underground'. The legislation that aimed to bring prostitution into the open has had the reverse effect. It is out of sight, out of mind. It is also out of control.

Escort agency work can be dangerous: clients can become violent and women do not have the 'minders' as most brothels do. It is the same, perhaps worse, for street prostitutes, who find robbery and rape an occupational hazard. In legal brothels, women might be safer, but the trade is not necessarily lucrative. The Prostitutes Collective says some women can work a 12-hour shift and take home only $40, out of which they have to pay taxi fares. They get no sick leave, no holiday pay, and may have to work in unhealthy environments. The collective believes 'working women' need an award, a legally-recognised pay and conditions deal with employers.

The legal brothel scene also has its own intrigues. A monthly magazine called *The Shopper* details developments in the trade. The magazine also offers updates on the 'big business' of legal brothels, especially those for sale. Many are offered only as leasehold premises and prices start at around $300,000. Others have been offered for $1 million. In mid-

1990, one of the city's most luxurious brothels, the Daily Planet in Elsternwick, was withdrawn from sale. Its asking price was around $12 million and the advertising brochure said the business returned 'an excellent $1.7 million nett per annum'. Advertisements also appear for debt collectors specialising in bounced cheques and dishonoured credit card payments. One advert said: 'You don't have to wear this nonsense any more, call in the experts and turn your problems into cash.' It would be naive to expect the vice industry to be a clean, crime-free business. It has traditionally been a big money earner, where the strongest and smartest survive, and it is likely to remain that way. In legalising it, new problems have been created and, in reality, the situation has not improved. The Prostitutes Collective believes things have got worse. The vice industry restructure has left fewer women in brothels, and more in escort agencies, leaving women more vulnerable to violent clients and those who refuse to wear condoms.

Legal brothel owners can do pretty much what they like and not lose their permits. They are the big men of the business and the only 'legitimate' people. Just about every other form of prostitution remains illegal. Probably the biggest flaw is the lack of a body to oversee the industry. Neave suggested that a three-member board be established to grant and review permits; it would have the power to cancel a permit without a hearing. Since the first brothel was granted its permit in 1984, there has been no such body. Pubs and nightclubs need to satisfy the Liquor Control Commission that they are fit to hold a licence. Penalties can be imposed and the renewal of licences denied if a business is involved in trading outside hours, drug dealing, violence and allowing under-age clients on premises. A similar operation was envisaged for the brothel industry, but with tougher powers and regulations, to ensure that criminality, disease, workers and customers under 18, and drugs were kept out of brothels. The board was to use police to act as its investigators and, in turn, would act as a watchdog of police abuse.

When the Liberals said they wanted all prostitutes licensed and overseen by the board, the Cain administration abandoned half its legislation, including a section that would have allowed police entry into a legal brothel at any reasonable time, and a section creating a board of control. Only local council officers can now enter brothels to check that everything is in order, as brothels have been relegated simply to a local government planning matter. If they choose, council officers can ask police to accompany them. The Municipal Officers' Association, which represents by-law officers, said they were just not qualified or equipped to do the job. There have also been reports of officers being bribed to turn a blind eye to, for example, late-night opening. Local councils, which continue to get complaints from residents about noise and other problems, could have referred matters to the board: as it stands now, they can do very little.

Some argue that police should be kept out of brothels because of the potential for corruption, an argument borne out by the revelations of free sex, bribes and protection money given to police during Queensland's Fitzgerald Inquiry. In Victoria, the Government agreed that police were the best people to monitor brothels; having the experience, numbers and an in-built system to investigate corruption and, if all of the proposed laws could have been enacted, a board of control would have been able to oversee both the police and brothel activity. Under the emasculated legislation, police have to stay out of brothels unless they raid a building with a warrant.

By early 1990, there were 59 legal brothels in Melbourne and a number of others awaiting permits. Who owned them was anyone's guess. Certainly police, the government or local councils have not been able to answer the question. The original legislation would have required owners to identify themselves, but that did not become law. Most brothels are owned by companies, and changes in directors are hard to keep up with. Once one includes cross-company shareholdings, the ownership question becomes a hopeless maze. The law requires that permit holders must not have a serious recent criminal record. It also says no one can hold more than one permit. But the ownership maze allows all sorts of abuse. Multiple ownership has certainly happened – and gone unpunished – and the use of 'front men' in the company structures allows anyone to own a legal brothel, irrespective of prior convictions.

Under the original legislation, permits would have lasted three years. A change in ownership would have required the board's consent for a brothel's operations to continue. Some brothels have had an indefinite permit granted to them. More recent applications have had time limits imposed, such as three years, after which the permit needs to be renewed. But permits are for the building not the applicant. This means buildings can be sold and the new 'owner' need only have, at worst, a relatively clean criminal record to take over an operation.

Police are convinced front men are acting as 'owners' for criminal groups. Money made from drug trafficking easily passes through the brothel accounts to become legitimate.

What the Government passed was a tattered collection of ideas that has failed to monitor the 'legal' side of the vice industry, and does not even address escort agencies, a scene that in the 1980s has seen the violence of standover men, a crop of bashings and at least four murders.

The flesh trade is still open to criminal abuse, corruption, exploitation and coercion, and rather than making it open and accountable, the laws have pushed more of it underground. The original aim of the law was four-fold: to protect the young from exploitation; protect adult prostitutes from violence and intimidation; protect the community from nuisance and disturbance; and establish adequate controls over the operators and managers of brothels. It has clearly failed.

7
Illegal Gambling

Victorians love a punt. Whether on the races, a televised lottery or an electronic machine, they are very quick to hand their money over for a flutter. History has shown that they have never been too worried if the bet was legal or not. Illegal betting has been a feature of Victoria since first settlement, and police corruption has been its almost constant bed partner. It took police 14 years to finally close John Wren's infamous Collingwood tote in 1907.

The gaming area has always been the Victorian police force's Achilles heel. In modern times, there have been four memorable times when honest police have been brought in to clean up the gaming squad: Mick Miller in the 1950s; Fred Silvester in the early 1970s, Bob Pittaway in the early 1980s and Peter Halloran in the late 1980s. In 1956, when Chief Commissioner Major General Selwyn Porter was faced with a large number of police being paid by illegal starting price bookmakers, he sacked the entire gaming squad and formed a smaller group of young police. It was named the special duties gaming squad, and consisted of men with no previous affiliation in that area.

The man chosen as operational head of the strike force was an almost unknown senior constable from the Richmond police station, Mick Miller, who would one day become Chief Commissioner. Miller's direct boss, Inspector M. J. Healey, was an honest cop who would not be silenced. Healey later told a Royal Commission into off-course betting that when he took over in 1956, about 30 per cent of police involved in gaming investigations were corrupt, 20 per cent were inefficient and only 50 per cent did a reasonable job. Under cross examination, he agreed that this meant about 800 police throughout the State had accepted bribes in the gaming area. He also said that after the Miller clean-up operation, the gaming squad was free of corruption for the first time in 30 years. He said some members of the old gaming squad used to protect their protection of SP bookmakers by refusing promotion, to avoid having to leave the squad. Healey warned, prophetically, that if the right type of police were not kept in the gaming area 'the rot will set in'.

The special duties gaming squad made many enemies among corrupt police, some of whom later rose to high ranks and positions of enormous influence. Miller's squad, which obtained its raiding warrants at the Russell Street press rooms from *Herald* crime reporter Alan Dower, who was also a Justice of the Peace, attacked a huge illegal industry that had also corrupted elements within the then Postmaster-General's Department (PMG) over telephone installation. Criticism of links between the PMG, and its successor Telecom, with the SP industry were repeated in the early 1980s and again in 1990. Miller's group was largely responsible for two judicial inquiries. The first, headed by Justice Martin in 1958, resulted in the TAB being established. The second, headed by Justice Taylor in 1962, found a large number of improper practices in the PMG. (In 1984, a Melbourne QC, Frank Vincent (now a Supreme Court judge), headed a further inquiry into allegations of questionable practices in Telecom. He found there was no evidence that organised crime had infiltrated Telecom, but severely criticised the body for not pursuing wrongdoing by staff.)

In 1971 – by which time Miller had been promoted to Assistant Commissioner, and was again concerned with the running of the gaming, licensing and vice squads – one of the original members of his team from the 1950s, Fred Silvester, was chosen to put a new broom through the area. A new crackdown was launched against not only SP bookmakers, but also illegal casinos, baccarat and other forms of illegal betting. One SP bookmaker who moved out of the way to Queensland was called 'Tweety Bird' – the one Silvester could not catch.

In the early 1970s, a well-spoken, personable Queensland policeman travelled to Victoria to discuss SP bookmakers. He told police in Melbourne he wanted information on the illegal bookmaking industry for further investigations when he returned to Brisbane. Senior Victorian police were impressed with his attitude and provided confidential information, including names of SP bookmakers in Queensland linked to their inquiries. The Queensland policeman took dossiers and promised immediate action. Police in Victoria were disappointed to learn that nothing was done. The Queenslander was Jack Herbert, the man who was later shown by the Fitzgerald inquiry to have been on the take for years.

By the early 1980s, the rot also had set in again in Victoria. An investigation found serious corruption in the gaming branch. According to a report published in the *Age* on 29 October 1984, many cases had been faked and the books fixed to make it look as though SP bookmakers had been prosecuted when, in fact, the cases had been withdrawn. In a replica of the action taken by Porter in 1956, Chief Commissioner Miller set up a task force, code-named Zebra, which not only purged the gaming squad, but also blitzed protected SP bookmakers.

Still the spectre of bribery persisted. In 1988, after police intelligence again indicated that some gambling figures were being protected in Victoria, a new crackdown was ordered under Chief Inspector Peter Halloran. And again suspect members were moved from the gaming squad. New methods of security were introduced to avoid leaks to gambling figures.

A report brought down by Queensland's Criminal Justice Commission (CJC) in 1990 pointed to massive SP networks right throughout Australia, which relied on corruption among public officials. The CJC estimated Australia-wide SP bookmaking to be worth $6000 million a year. The report raised renewed questions about Telecom's role in SP bookmaking, and the racing industry's passive acceptance of illegal betting. While most media publicity on organised crime concentrates on drugs, fraud and illegal corporate activities, the area of gambling remains a massive fund-raiser for crime figures. In Victoria alone the figures are staggering. The multi-million dollar SP industry is well known, but each day in the State huge amounts are gambled by everyone from school children to businessmen.

Video poker machines that have mushroomed around Carlton and Brunswick make massive profits every day. Police estimate at least 300 of the machines operate in that area alone and thousands around the State. Police know that machines in good locations make between $500 and $1000 a day profit. They say some of the machines are finding their way into hotels. A conservative estimate is that all the illegal machines in Victoria pull about $200,000 a day in profit. Estimates on annual profits from the machines vary from $70 million to $100 million.

According to Tom Noble's book *Untold Violence*, an Italian in Carlton has become a millionaire from his involvement in the machines. He has also been connected with a known gunman in an illegal casino in North Fitzroy that was raided and closed by police. Police have not been able to dent the illegal video machine industry because cumbersome legislation makes it difficult to act, and because of sophisticated technology. Cafe owners use remote control devices so the machine is turned to a harmless amusement device whenever police enter the premises. Some machines are also designed to destroy the illegal computer program when they are opened up, making it difficult for police to gather evidence of illegal gambling.

Four illegal casinos operate in Melbourne's Chinatown, and big gamblers are legendary, with huge lines of credit being offered to known big punters. Police intelligence has established that massive amounts of drug money move through the gambling houses. Turnover of more than $100,000 at a single den is not unusual. Police estimate that $250,000 can change hands in the Chinatown dens on the big night of the week – Sunday, the night when Asian restaurants close early. Individual patrons have been known to lose $60,000 in an evening. On one occasion, six Chinese heroin dealers from Sydney sold large amounts of drugs to Melbourne wholesalers and then went to one of the games in Chinatown. They arrived carrying at least $150,000 stuffed in paper bags.

Each den is protected with huge steel doors and video camera surveillance designed to thwart police operations. A patron wanting to attend one of the houses would first be checked by an external camera. If he was acceptable, the external steel door would be opened electronically. The patron then climbs a set of stairs where he would again be checked by a second camera before another steel door would open, giving him access to the gambling area. Between 40 and 70 gamblers, nearly all Asian, attend each club at night.

During a major crackdown by police on Chinatown gambling in 1989, Peter Halloran and another officer, Stephen Pierce, were offered more than $125,000 each a year to protect two gambling dens. They were to receive $2000 each week, plus bonuses on big nights, to lay off the two clubs. The men who made the offer were charged, but the maximum penalty for bribery in Victoria is only $400. In previous bribe attempts that resulted in charges, police were offered $500 to $600 a week. There have been attempts by Asian criminals to stand over the gambling interests, and investigators have been hampered by the traditional Chinese reluctance to complain to police.

Not that the Chinese have a monopoly on illegal gambling houses. In busy Lygon Street, Carlton, at least two well-fortified dens have catered for Australian–Italian criminals. Police have estimated about $100,000 changes hands on a busy night at the clubs. Behind the steel doors, drug dealers, armed robbers and standover men mingle and bet. Many major crimes are hatched at the clubs. In one incident, two criminals confronted a man in one of the Lygon Street dens to settle an old score. Guns were drawn and a former boxer bodyguard was ordered not to become involved while the debt was settled. The victim was forced to sit in a chair while he was methodically pistol-whipped and bashed until he was in a coma. Even though the victim nearly died, he refused to talk to police when he had recovered. He was bashed because a criminal gang blamed him for police being called to another violent incident several years earlier.

Authorities have maintained that it is impossible to give definitive figures on illegal gambling turnover in the State, but they estimate that with SP betting, video machines and Melbourne's gambling dens, between $1 million and $2.5 million would be illegally wagered every day. None of the money is taxed, and the loss in Government revenue is massive.

Police themselves have argued that the Government must provide legal and competitive alternatives to illegal betting, but warn that, if the Government takes too much in taxes, punters will return to illegal alternatives because they can receive a greater return for their investment. It is impossible, they say, for police to stamp out illegal betting without legal alternatives for punters. The iron law of crime is that where there is a demand there will be a supply. Police know that large amounts of the gambling profits are ploughed into the drug industry.

In 1982, the Cain Government decided to explore the possibility of introducing legal casinos. It appointed a former Federal Court judge, Xavier Connor, QC, to head a board of inquiry on the casino issue. The Government was embarrassed during the inquiry when the then Minister for Economic Development, Bill Landeryou, said despite 'some difficulties with a particular judge' he hoped Victoria would get a casino. Connor asserted his independence, even ignoring an official police submission, which recommended that Victoria should get casinos. The police submission said: 'If the gaming needs of a population are not met legally, a series of illegal gambling ventures occurs and grows to meet the demand. Providing a legal means for local people and visitors to gamble might, therefore, on balance, be in the best interests of good order from a law enforcement agency's point of view.' Police said they favoured casinos like Wrest Point in Hobart. 'There would be no objection if such a casino complex was introduced, providing strict controls and effective legislation complemented its introduction.'

Connor, however, took more notice of others, particularly an individual Victorian policeman, Michael Schuett, who was attached to the Bureau of Criminal Intelligence. Consulted regularly by interstate and overseas law enforcement bodies, he liaised with the Connor inquiry on the facts of organised criminal life in Victoria. Schuett was granted Australian law enforcement's highest honour – the Australian Police Medal – before he resigned from the force in 1989. His farewell was attended by judges, parliamentarians and grateful confidants from around Australia

Connor's report opposed casinos on the basis that he believed they may be infiltrated by organised crime. When tabling the Connor report, Cain told Parliament on 24 May 1983: 'The Government is not prepared to expose this State and its citizens to the avoidable risk of introducing a facility upon which organised crime could prosper.' Cain also made it clear that Connor had rejected the police submission. 'The Board concluded that the confidence of certain police witnesses as to their ability to control organised crime was misplaced.'

After John Cain resigned as Premier in 1990, his successor, Joan Kirner, wasted no time in announcing, in December 1990, a somersault on Connor's recommendations. It was decided to approve *two* legal casinos. Andrew Lamb, a director of Hospitality and Leisure Enterprises Pty Ltd, and who provides market studies for casinos, told the *Sunday Herald* that turnover from Melbourne casinos could be $240 to $340 million a year and possibly more.

8
Illegal Drugs

For most of this century, prostitution and illegal gambling have been the steady businesses for Victoria's leading criminals. In the mid-1970s things changed; drugs arrived. The effects have been enormous: a new, more vicious style of criminal has evolved; police have battled against a surge in crime; the State's prisons have filled; there has been an untold cost in suffering and medical care; and the huge amount of money available in the drug trade has led to more police corruption. What started with an upsurge in heroin and marijuana use, then later amphetamine and cocaine, has in some way affected thousands of Victorian families.

Statistics support the common perception that crime is worse than a decade ago: burglaries, car theft and robberies occur about twice as often as they did 10 years ago. More Victorians know someone who has been a victim, a witness or involved in an investigation in some way. Melburnians also feel their city is not as safe as it was a decade ago. A survey published in the *Sunday Age* in early 1991 showed that nine per cent of people thought the city was safer than 10 years earlier; more than 70 per cent said it was less safe. What proportion of the crime increase is directly due to drugs is anyone's guess (police have estimated that 80 per cent of crime is 'drug-related'). There is little doubt, however, that drugs have had a big influence.

Certainly their arrival has changed Melbourne's crime scene. The vast financial rewards in drug dealing have lured thousands of people into Victoria's drug trade. To protect their drug empires, some criminals are extremely violent, with many disputes settled by bashings and murders. More criminals are carrying guns and knives than a decade ago. And the crimes committed by addicts to sustain their habits have fuelled multi-million dollar rackets in stolen goods.

Despite the doubling of the crime rate in the past decade, the number of detectives in the force has increased by less than 30 per cent, and detectives still make up just over 10 per cent of all police. Some police complain that for sophisticated criminals, Melbourne's 'Mr Big Enoughs', it is becoming easier and easier to escape detection. The enormous increase in the police workload means that more crimes are simply not investigated, or only looked at briefly. It is no surprise that the solution rate for crimes is down. Drugs cost the community in many other ways, including: the need to house thousands of prisoners convicted of drug crimes; the medical complications of drug addiction, such as AIDS and hepatitis; and the corruption of public officials.

Drug abuse is not new to Australia. Heroin, morphine and cocaine, usually sold in pharmaceutical products such as cough medicine, took off in popularity in the 1880s through mass marketing by unscrupulous pharmaceutical companies. Their strategy, according to Alfred McCoy's book *Drug Traffic*, involved 'an appealing brand name, narcotic or alcohol content, and massive fraudulent advertising'. Many contained morphine, heroin or cocaine, and they sold in huge amounts. In the early 1900s, attempts were made to stamp out the use of non-medicinal opium, most of which was used in opium dens frequented by Chinese. As a result of a campaign best noted for its racism, a black market replaced the legal importation of opium and the price dropped. (Victoria's opium dens died out in the 1960s as older Chinese, the last generation of smokers, died off.)

But the sale of drug-rich medicines through grocers, and pure heroin and cocaine through chemists, thrived. After the First World War, many diggers returned home as cocaine addicts, and cocaine became the big postwar drug. Attempts to stamp it out led black markets to spring up, with huge amounts of cocaine sold by immoral chemists. Violence in Melbourne and Sydney over control of the drug market followed. By the mid-1930s, Australia had the highest per capita consumption of cocaine, morphine and heroin in the Western world.

The trade, however, dropped off during the Second World War and never returned to its original level. In the 1950s and 1960s, there was a surge in the sale of barbiturates and amphetamines – tranquillisers and stimulants – mostly sold as over the counter products. But in the late 1960s a new culture emerged and, following trends in Europe, drugs such as marijuana, amphetamines and LSD became increasingly popular. About the same time, there was a second big surge in the world heroin trade, fuelled by the war in Vietnam. Heroin began coming to Australia in increasing quantities, initially much of it with United States servicemen who took leave in Australia. In the mid-1970s, domestic heroin use mushroomed; some analysts attributed this to the end of the Vietnam war and the need for Asian heroin producers to find new markets to replace the US servicemen users.

As domestic heroin use grew, Australian authorities concentrated much of their efforts on Australian crime gangs involved in drugs, especially in smuggling. The Chinese community in Australia – members of which have imported the drug in small quantities for decades, mainly for a tiny population of opium and heroin users – was significantly under-policed, something law enforcement officials later conceded was a mistake. Privately, National Crime Authority investigators say Chinese groups are now responsible for importing 75 per cent of Australia's heroin, and some consider that the proportion is as high as 90 per cent. Considering the number of individual operators and other groups involved in the heroin trade, this figure is likely to be too high. The 75 per cent figure may also be over-inflated. The problem is that no one will ever know the amount Chinese groups import into Australia, primarily because there is no accurate figure of total heroin consumption.

In 1978, a federal Royal Commission on drug trafficking, conducted by Mr Justice Williams, estimated that between 900 and 1300 kilograms of heroin was needed to supply Australia's addicts. Today, most estimates of the annual requirement start at 1000 kilograms, although some believe it to be far less. Accepting that 1000 kilograms of heroin comes into Australia each year makes the activities of even the much-publicised 'Mr Asia' gang, which imported about 70 kilograms of the drug over three years, seem rather insignificant. The problem is that no one knows how many Australians use heroin. There have been estimates of 20,000 regular heroin users. Figures released by the Federal Government's National Campaign Against Drug Abuse, put the number of 'regular dependent heroin users' at between 30,000 and 50,000. Whatever the estimates, Chinese groups, especially those in Sydney, play a key role in heroin importation. Big seizures in the late 1980s proved that. They import heroin in bulk and are able to create good stockpiles. This means that seizures have little, if any, effect on market supply, or on the purity of heroin at street level.

Heroin comes into Australia in a multitude of ways: by ship, in shipping containers, by air and parcel post. And the rewards are huge. One kilogram of top-grade heroin costs up to $10,000 in Bangkok. (It can also be bought in other Asian cities, but much of the heroin from the Golden Triangle, the source for most of Australia's heroin, goes through Bangkok.)

In Australia it is sold at wholesale level for around $140,000 a kilogram. At this stage the drug is uncut, often round 90 per cent pure, and can be cheaper if bought in bulk. It is then sold on for up to $200,000 (often interstate), at which point a dealer will start diluting it and selling ounce-size lots for $5000 or $6000. The dealer who buys at this level is sometimes a drug user. He will further dilute the drug (sometimes by half, therefore producing two ounces) and sell it for about $200 a gram. The particulars may vary; more or fewer dealers may be involved.

While Melbourne's Chinese criminals play second-fiddle to their Sydney counterparts, they are still strongly involved in the drug trade. One man, who has run illegal Chinese gambling clubs in Melbourne, often travels with bodyguards and has a love of punting big at the races. He is believed to have lost a large amount of money he invested in a heroin shipment when police seized a huge consignment that was hidden on a boat. Melbourne has at least three other Chinese crime groups involved in wholesale heroin dealing. One appears to be the Melbourne 'branch' of a Sydney crime group. Leading figures in each group never touch the drugs themselves. Three of these Melbourne groups have strong links to illegal gambling, prostitution, large-scale fraud and immigration rackets. Like all organised criminals, they use junior employees to do the dirty work – and in Melbourne that often means Vietnamese youths.

In recent years, an increasing number of Vietnamese criminals – some of whom work in Chinese gambling clubs – have become involved in heroin distribution down to street level. Some brutal disputes involving guns, knives and meat cleavers have focused media attention on this trend, but it is important to note that, despite these incidents, the Vietnamese community in Australia has one of the lowest crime rates per head of any ethnic population. And while Chinese criminals dominate the importation of heroin, other groups distribute the drugs. Some groups run along ethnic lines – Greeks, Italians, Rumanians, Lebanese and Anglo-Australians – while others are groups of mixed origin. Many of these also trade in amphetamines, cocaine and marijuana.

Heroin, however, is the most pernicious of the illegal drugs. It is addictive, expensive and is sold on the streets, where poverty is greatest. Money to buy the drugs commonly comes from burglaries, theft from cars, shoplifting, armed robbery and prostitution, while money to buy cocaine often comes from legitimate sources of income. Apart from the financial cost created by heroin-related crime, there are the social and medical complications: heroin addicts rarely hold down a job, many inject the drug under conditions of poor hygiene and many readily become ill. Some contract hepatitis or AIDS. Likewise, amphetamines pose huge health risks. This stimulant, sometimes known as 'the poor man's cocaine', is taken orally (mixed with a drink such as Coca-Cola), inhaled through the nose, or mixed in a solution and injected.

In the mid-1960s, some 30 years after the drug was first marketed as Benzedrine, amphetamines surged in popularity. 'Mods' picked up their purple hearts, students used them to cram for exams and truck drivers kept awake all night on long-haul routes, fired up by a few pills. In the late 1960s, Australian governments, alarmed by the rise in amphetamine use, reclassified the drug, which effectively banned it from general use. A lucrative black market quickly sprang up, but tastes changed, and the drug's popularity faded. Some of those black marketeers moved into the marijuana and heroin trades. Amphetamines, however, kept their popularity among motorbike gangs, where alcohol and amphetamines were part of the culture. Both were good for partying, and amphetamines, which gave the user a feeling of well-being, excitement, exhilaration and energy, stimulated individuals to be racy and active. In the early 1980s, members of the Melbourne chapter of the Hell's Angels Motorcycle Club visited the United States and learned how to produce amphetamines. After importing the ingredients, club members began manufacturing the pure, crystal form of the drug at a house in Wattle Glen, north-east of Melbourne. Their initial product was dispersed among the motorcycle fraternity, but as they began to make more and more amphetamine, the drug found its way to new, eager markets. In effect, the members of the Hell's Angels established a market that exploded in the late 1980s, prompting Victoria's police to describe the problem as the State's biggest drug threat.

Methylamphetamine, the crystal form of the amphetamine group, is the most potent form of the drug. It is made under simple laboratory conditions, requiring only the chemicals, a knowledge of basic chemistry, running water and electricity to produce. It sells for around $1100 a ounce, more than twice the price of gold. Like heroin, it is generally diluted with glucose or a similar powder, and is sold in small amounts wrapped in silver foil, usually $50 for less than a gram. For the user of the late 1980s, it kept the body active for hours at nightclubs: it also negated some of the effects of heavy drinking. Although the manufacture needs to be precise (one mistake can ruin the process), its production is relatively quick. In 12 hours a small laboratory can be set up, the drugs made and packed, and the whole lab then dismantled and perhaps packed into the boot of a car, which can make finding laboratories very difficult for police.

Combining the necessary chemicals poses two main threats, apart from the ever-present danger of making an error. One is toxic fumes, the other is heat generated by one of the reactions – heat capable of causing an explosion big enough to wreck a laboratory and kill anyone in it. For these reasons, the drug is often produced in country areas. For the Hell's

Angels, the drugs precipitated a violent split within the group in the mid-1980s, which saw bashings, shootings and the expulsion of club members. Although police suspect the Angels still have influence in the amphetamine market, their domination of the early 1980s is long gone. New techniques and ingredients have made the production process easier. Criminals involved in the marijuana and heroin trade have found that, with a small investment, there are big rewards. Professional armed robbers have also moved into the amphetamine trade, finding the chances of getting caught are less, while the gains are just as good, if not better. Since the Hell's Angels began mass marketing amphetamines in early 1981, the manufacturing know-how has spread throughout Australia. Today, Melbourne alone has more than 20 criminal groups capable of making the drug called 'speed'.

Cocaine also made a resurgence in the late 1980s, but not to the extent seen in the 1920s, or to the extent predicted by some law enforcement authorities. It wasn't until 1983 that Australian enforcement authorities received their first firm wholesale price quotation on multi-kilogram cocaine consignments. Depending on the amount wanted, the quote was $60,000 to $140,000 a kilogram. This, and subsequent 'quotes' to undercover police, combined with the awesome amounts of cocaine flooding into the United States, left many Australians believing our turn would come in 1986 or 1987. It didn't, and the emergence of 'crack' in many American cities has since been used to explain a delay in the drug's arrival.

Crack, basically cocaine mixed with baking soda and cooked in an oven for a few hours, has caused serious health and social problems in America. A piece of crack costs about $10 and, when smoked, gives the euphoric effect of cocaine. Some people argue that the emergence of crack in America opened up the new, and huge, market of the poor and underprivileged. While they were unable to meet the price tag of cocaine, they could afford crack. Colombian cartels happily increased their production to supply the new market.

One of the first detailed pictures of a big cocaine syndicate operating in Australia emerged after a series of police investigations that began in 1987. It established that a group of Colombian-born men were importing at least six kilograms a month hidden in frozen food, impregnated in clothing and diluted in liquids. Police think some came in containers, although most came by couriers on regular commercial flights. Most of the drug came into Sydney, the headquarters of the operation. The Melbourne end of the Colombian group sold cocaine to Greek, Italian and Australian criminals, including several former members of the Painters and Dockers' Union and a well-known Italian gambling identity.

Police have evidence that the group was given instructions by senior members in Colombia, who received profits in the form of legitimate money. One of the main figures at the Sydney end of the syndicate fled to Colombia when he became aware of police inquiries. With a kilogram of cocaine costing $US10,000 wholesale in New York, and its price in Sydney or Melbourne $A140,000, the attraction to smugglers is obvious. It is likely more cocaine will find its way to Australia.

The drug boom since the mid to late 1970s has brought with it a different style of criminal. Older police talk about the 'understanding' and 'rules' that were once adhered to by criminals and police, a type of grudging mutual admiration. Nowadays there is more violence and animosity between police and criminals, demonstrated in one way by the surge in shootings between the two groups in the late 1980s. It is clear now that few, if any, rules exist. And like drug dealing anywhere, at all levels it is a dangerous business.

There have been scores of drug-related murders in Victoria in the past decade, and many people have simply disappeared. Homicide squad detectives have several times searched an area of bush near Kinglake, north of Melbourne, where a number of bodies are supposed have been buried during the 1980s; not one has been found. Some murders are especially brutal, and are preceded by torture and mutilation, but the killings are only the tip of the iceberg when it comes to violence. Those in the business have to protect their empires from any threat: opposition groups taking over, police informants, rip-offs, and bad debts. Dozens of armed robberies and brutal assaults go unreported each year, as those in Victoria's drug trade settle disputes, steal from each other, or give savage 'warnings' to those who owe money or who are suspected of talking to police.

An example of a violent drug dealer was Dennis Allen, a leading distributor of heroin and amphetamines in Melbourne from 1983 to 1987. His drug turnover in 1984 was a minimum of $17,500 a week, and probably much more. By the end of 1984 he had bought 10 houses in Richmond, then spent tens of thousands more on renovations. He often carried thousands of dollars stuffed down the front of his bib-and-brace overalls. Allen used friends and family members to protect an empire that grew at an astonishing rate. In the five years that Allen's business was operating, dozens of people were savagely bashed and at least half a dozen murdered. Allen was directly involved in several of the murders, including one in which he chopped off the legs of his victim with a chainsaw. The motives for all the murders are not clear, although one killing was of a suspected police informer and another was related to a bad debt.

Allen's drug dealing and violence attracted the attention of police, but often he appeared to have advance knowledge of any investigations. He boasted of contacts with corrupt police and once claimed that he paid $25,000 for the details of one particular police inquiry. The involvement of corrupt police in Victoria's drug trade has been a leading concern for senior police in recent years. Unlike corruption in the vice and gambling areas, where the rewards are relatively small, drugs are big business. Illegal gambling and prostitution are also looked on by some as victimless crimes – in other words, those who participate do so willingly and harm no one in the greater community. But drugs are more evil – they lead to death, misery for addicts and cost dearly in crime, medical care, and police, prison and social welfare resources.

The common perception among Victorians is that their police are relatively clean and preferable to their NSW or Queensland counterparts. While this faith is well founded, it is not to say that corruption among Victoria's police is uncommon. However, most of those caught have been renegades, and there is no evidence of any organised structure with high-level police authorisation, as has been seen in Queensland. Certainly, many drug shipments go through other States because of the perception by criminals that Melbourne has a cleaner force: it is easier to arrange a different point of entry. This is boosted by the successes of the Federal Police and Australian Customs Service in seizing drugs in Victoria. In other States, particularly NSW, there is more rivalry between the services – and less success.

Corruption comes in many forms: police can 'assist' certain drug dealers by enthusiastically investigating – and removing – the competition. It can be providing information to criminals about the progress of police inquiries, information that can – and does – destroy months of detective work. Police involved in raids and arrests often discover thousands of dollars of cash and drugs, and for some the temptation is too much. Some police can be directly involved in drug distribution. One such officer was William Harris, a detective with 25 years in the force, who became involved in a plot to import 330 kilograms of cannabis resin (hashish) through Melbourne Airport. Harris 'arranged' for a senior customs officer to clear the illicit cargo and, for his help, was to receive $50,000, more than twice his annual after-tax salary. Harris was caught after months of work by Federal and Victorian Police, following a tip-off by an informer. The key evidence against him came from telephone taps. These revealed, at one point, that Harris had been tipped off by a colleague about the supposedly secret inquiry. Harris was convicted of conspiracy and sentenced to 14 years in jail.

In 1985 the Victoria Police doubled the size of its internal investigations department and established the internal security unit, a separate group that initiates inquiries into suspected police criminality – especially in the area of drug trafficking – rather than just responding to public complaints. It uses all the powers and tricks available to it, including surveillance, bugs and telephone taps. In 1990 the unit began a major investigation, code-named Operation Clare, into police believed to have 'sold out' a number of big drug inquiries. But crooked police are clever, they know the tricks of the trade and they know how to beat them. Although senior officers often have a strong belief that a policeman may be corrupt, little can be done without proof. For years, the former Chief Commissioner, Mick Miller, pleaded for the power to sack errant police. He knew who was corrupt, but the system meant little could be done without sufficient proof to satisfy a court of law. Miller's pleas were rejected.

The changes that drugs have brought to Victoria since the early 1970s have been enormous – and the biggest problem facing the community is what to do about illegal drugs. Prohibition has failed to stop or even seriously hinder the drug trafficking, and the options of decriminalising or legalising drug use have only started to be seriously canvassed. In two decades the problem has only got worse and it is likely, if nothing is done, that the drug problem will continue to deteriorate through the 1990s.

9

Illegal Privilege

As a lawyer, Frank Butera eschewed criminal law. On the surface, he exuded the aura of just another up-and-coming Melbourne solicitor making his way doing conveyancing and commercial work. Behind the facade, he was a criminal lawyer – in the illegal sense.

Unpublicised by the media of Melbourne, the story of Frank Butera provides a hidden insight into the parasitic nature of elements of the Victorian legal profession. From the supposed sanctuary of his legal practice, Butera dealt in illicit drugs. Knowing full well the legal difficulty in proving anything unless caught with drugs in his possession, Butera made sure that he never personally touched the stuff. Butera's undoing resulted from an undercover operation by the Australian Federal Police, using their legal power to intercept telephones for drug trafficking offences.

Sentenced in November 1986 (along with four others) to 11 years in jail, Butera thought that, being a lawyer, his phone would have been immune, especially with powerful sections of the legal profession in Victoria leading the public lobby against police being able to tap phones. Presented with intelligence material gathered by the AFP's Melbourne drug unit, a judge formally approved the placing of an intercept on a phone used by Butera in the office of his legal practice, as well as a phone used by one of his drug contacts. The AFP knew that Butera was involved in drug dealings with a syndicate of Indians operating out of Thailand, Singapore and Malaysia. The Indians had come to notice through their association with a suspect travel agency.

When the AFP began the tapping operation in July 1983, Butera was dealing almost daily with one of the syndicate members living in Melbourne and awaiting word from another who had gone to Asia. Excerpts from the tapes give a revealing account of the shadowy connections of Melbourne's drug underworld. On 7 July 1983, within hours of the first tap being put in place, Butera received a call from Gurdap Singh, nicknamed 'Goodie'.

Singh: 'Yeah, er, you remember you told me before on the phone that, er, you organised you made arrangements for the last 20 G?'

Butera: 'Yeah, I have. I need to take possession of it on Friday. But the, ahhm, the money will be given to me at a later stage. Probably a week after or whatever, there's no hassle. It's not the same people, they're not interested in that amount.'

When Singh rang in the next day, Butera greeted him as 'counsellor'.

Singh: 'It's all on. You see, I told you I was hearing from my side today. Yeah, it's all on.'

Butera: 'Well, Goodie, listen, how, how do I get half of my money?'

Singh: 'I put it all into his accounts here [referring to accounts held by Navin Kumara, the partner who had gone overseas to organise another consignment]. I banked it.'

Butera: 'You're fuckin' joking.'

Singh: 'No.'

Butera: 'When you talk to him, you tell him I want my half now.'

Later, faced with bills for a $1200 telephone account and other bills for a flat maintained in Melbourne for their overseas contact, Singh in a series of calls continually pressed

Butera to advance him money from payments still due from a Melbourne distributor.

Butera: 'See, what it is, I gave it to him, right, and he sells it individually. But he's okay, because I've dealt with him in the past. Navin [overseas contact] knows him. I'll try to rustle this guy up. And I'll make sure I got something for you.'

Singh: 'All right, yeah, yeah.'

Butera: 'I'd use mine, but it's stashed away. It's not worth the hassle, you know what I mean?'

Singh: 'All right, yeah, yeah.'

Butera: 'Not that I've got any fears of, um, advancing the money. I would, but it's just awkward to get to. You're a fool for banking it all, anyhow.'

Singh: 'I'm regretting [it] myself. I'm personally and, ah, quite desperate. I'm calling you not because I don't trust you. If I didn't trust you, I wouldn't have handed you the stuff without the money.'

Butera: 'No, don't worry, don't worry. If he doesn't call me, I'll step in and do something myself. If he doesn't call me, Navin knows who he is. He's reliable, there's no doubt about that. It's just a question of getting hold of him.'

When an associate rang reminding him about unpaid bills, Singh spoke of a million-dollar deal coming up. The bills were all 'due to what I'm trying to get through, that's all'.

Singh: 'You see, I've settled my side of it here. It's all organised. So that is why I have to spend the money getting my side organised and if I can get another deal through.'

Associate: 'Okay, all right.'

Singh: 'Okay, see you, bye, bye. Hey, don't open your mouth, all right?'

In the meantime, Butera had telephoned a fellow Italian called Ivan.

Butera: 'Listen, Iv [Ivan], I rang about the money, mate.'

Ivan: 'Um, can you give me about another week?'

Butera: 'Yeah. It's just that I bought a house. And I'm getting more together, save me sort [of] running around and pulling money back out.'

Ivan: 'Where did you get the house?'

Butera: 'In Moonee Ponds. I can spend in it as much as I like and no one will know the difference. You'll blow your mind, mate. It's beautiful. When I finish with it, it will be stunning.'

Ivan: 'Good one.'

Butera: 'What have you been up to, anyhow?'

Ivan: 'Nothing at all. I haven't done much, just, ah, keeping my nose clean.'

Butera: 'Best way to be, mate.'

Ivan: 'Oh, I don't know whether it's the best way to be, but at least I'm doing it. Trying to, anyway. It's pretty hard to make a dollar these days.'

Butera: 'Yeah, I know, mate. Not just for you, Ivan, for the majority. Ninety-nine per cent of the society is in the same boat, mate. No, it's not worthwhile. It cost me money staying here [in the legal practice].'

Ivan: 'So you are gonna split, are you?'

Butera: 'Oh, yeah. Oh, bigger and better things.'

Ivan: 'Yeah, and what are the big things happening?'

Butera: 'I'd say the end of August ... it's only round the corner.'

Ivan: 'Sounds good, mate.'

Butera: 'Yeah, next year something, settle right down, get into some serious business.'

Ivan: 'Why not, why not, mate. How's your partner going, anyway, all right?'

Butera: 'Well, he's overseas, mate. He's there working on a couple of things. He should get back by the end of this month, first week in August and, ah, then we just fly off mate. Just waiting for him to get back. Well, mate, my fucking profession took me fuckin' five years, you know, to get here. I'm not gonna throw it away.'

Ivan: 'So you've got to be careful, well, you know what you want, anyway.'

Butera: 'Oh, yeah. We are doing serious things, Iv.'

Ivan: 'We'll go slowly, mate, slowly, slowly and you'll be all right.'

Another Italian-speaking contact named Rocky telephoned Butera three days later.

Rocky: 'How are things, nothing?'

Butera: 'Nothing yet.'

Rocky: 'Things are going fuckin' bad, mate.'

Butera: 'But someone told me that there is a lot of stuff around.'

Rocky: 'That's what they tell me, but I can't seem to find anything, absolutely nothing. Ah, I heard that G—'s got some.'

Butera: 'No, I don't believe it.'

Rocky: 'He's got it, he's got it, Charlie said. Yeah, last night I saw Carlo. And he had a bit.'

Butera: 'No, I don't believe it, my friend.'

Rocky: 'Because Carlo let me see a bit, no.'

Butera: 'Yeah, and how is it, brown?'

Rocky: 'No, good white.'

Butera: 'I don't know. It's possible, but I remember that I talked to him two weeks ago and he said he wasn't doing anything because he was going to Italy ... Well, see, I am only waiting, Rock, because it's not convenient for me to do, huh, anything else.'

Rocky: 'Made the best money in Australia.'

Butera: 'Who?'

Rocky: 'Me.'

Butera: 'Even you, jeez, everyone's going to Italy.'

Rocky: 'I spoke with someone that maybe they will give

him 10 kilos there and they might make him bring 10 kilos here.'

Butera: 'Yeah, but be careful what you do, mate.'

Rocky: 'Oh, well, I will see if they bring it here. And, um, then I have to see because they want at least half of the money when they get here.'

Butera: 'It's a lot of money, my friend.'

Rocky: 'Maybe they will give it to us, eh, seventy thousand, seventy-eighty thousand a kilo.'

Butera: 'Jeez, there's a lot to earn there.'

Rocky: 'Oh, yeah. You earn double. Yeah, no worries, mate. We will all make money, no worries.'

Another associate nicknamed Manno rang, asking: 'Listen, now just listen and just answer me straight after when I finish ... where are you scoring from?'

Butera: 'Oh, you're joking, aren't you? Manno, all I can get you is a buyer, a big one. I can't get you a contact because we'll bring it in ourselves.'

Manno: 'Oh, all right, what do you mean when you can get me a buyer?'

Butera: 'Whatever you got, I can get rid of it for you, money up front.'

Manno: 'No, no, no, I'm looking for someone, to get it from, to score from.'

Butera: 'It all, it all depends what sort of quality, because the only thing I know that's available is pretty bad.'

Manno: 'Oh, I thought you might have had something, um, better going.'

Butera: 'No, mate. If you'd rang me about, um, two months ago I might have been able to help you.'

Manno: 'Do you know anyone we could get it from?'

Butera: 'Only, only what do you call it, inferior quality, mate. I can give you a name, mate. You can check it yourself, but I am telling you now it won't be worth your while.'

Manno: 'No, well, if it's not worthwhile I don't want to waste me time.'

Butera: 'Manno, don't get involved, mate. You know how dirty this business is becoming.'

Manno: 'Yeah, but Frank, you know when you got, um, need for money you have to do ... '

Butera: 'But Manno, listen to me, mate, for, for the risk you are taking, right, dealing with people you don't know – all right, you think you know – you don't know who they're behind, who is setting them up. It's ... it is too fuckin' dangerous, mate.'

Manno: 'That is why I rang you up. I thought maybe you had a contact. I don't want that quality. I want to, um, get pure off you.'

Butera: 'Manno, look, mate, without blowing my trumpet, if I can't get it, no one can get it.'

Two hours later, Manno again rang, again asking to be put onto whoever had heroin available.

Butera: 'No, mate, no. If I could, I would. Keep away from it, mate.'

Manno: 'It's easier said than done for you, you've made it.'

Butera: (Laughs)

Manno: 'You've made it and then you say get away from it.'

Butera: 'Oh, only because I know what's involved, mate.'

Manno: 'Yeah, well, you've got it first. You got your 10, 12, 15 whatever – you got 300,000.'

Butera: 'Don't exaggerate.'

Manno: 'Hey?'

Butera: 'Don't exaggerate.'

Manno: 'Well, whatever it was, Frank, you got it. You got yourself out of debt, that's the thing.'

Butera: 'Hmm.'

Manno: 'That's all I want it for.'

Butera: 'Listen, mate, you know what I'll do, right, um, by

the end of August, all right I help you out.'

Manno: 'In what way?'

Butera: 'Financially.'

Manno: 'No, Frank, no.'

Butera: 'No, no, fair is fair, mate, we're mates.'

Manno: 'I'd prefer to, um, try and get something going than to pull it out of your pocket. I'd rather get something set and get it going, you know, make it work for once.'

Butera: 'Oh, what I'll do, I'll wait until I'm in a position to sort of back up my word, right, and, ah, I'll just offer you what I think is fair and reasonable and we'll leave it at that.'

Manno: 'Why, what have you got your little fuckin' fingers...'

Butera: 'No, I'm not doing anything at the moment. I'm not doing anything at the moment, mate.'

Manno: 'Yeah, well, you got something whipping up.'

Butera: 'Na, nothing whipping up, mate.'

Manno: 'Why, you haven't started whipping it, you're going to whip it later.'

Butera: (Laughs) 'Nothing whipping, mate.'

Manno: 'Get fucked.'

Butera: 'Nothing whipped, I've done what I have had to do, mate. It's made me age 10 years, but it had to be done.'

Manno: 'Yeah, I got to age 10 years, too. I'd like to age 10 years.'

On 20 July, Butera telephoned a contact called Tony.

Butera: 'I just rang up to say hi. Actually, you know, why I did ring up though to, er, find out if there was any development in that far substance.'

Tony: 'There's some around.'

Butera: 'Mmmm.'

Tony: 'You know what I mean?'

Butera: 'Mmmm.'

Tony: 'Listen, you wouldn't have the, er, get, er, your hands on that recipe of that, ah.'

Butera: 'I could manage it.'

Tony: 'No, not that white, that other stuff, that hard stuff. I heard it's made locally.'

Butera: 'Oh, er, I can ask.'

Tony: 'Right, now, let's talk business. The other stuff's there, still. There's a coupla, ahm, say kilos of coffee around, not the quantity you're after.'

Butera: (Sighs) 'Huh.'

On 23 July, Singh got back to Butera, explaining that he had phoned the overseas contact, but could not say much because he had a 'funny feeling'.

Singh: 'We've got a code, you see. The weather is bad. Communication isn't possible over the phone.'

Butera: 'Mm.'

Singh: 'You get me? There is somebody around. The weather is bad. He couldn't talk.'

Butera: 'You keep in touch with me, anyhow, on a daily basis.'

On 27 July, Butera got a call from a man called Larry.

Larry: 'It's me, mate. He rang me from up there. I didn't want to talk too much on the phone, you know.'

Butera: 'Um.'

Larry: 'But he's coming down. It's just not quite ready, he said, you know, but evidently it's there, just have to be patient, mate.'

Butera: 'Mmm, well, we'll just have to persevere with it, mate.'

On 28 July, Butera spoke to a man he referred to as Abraham.

Butera: 'I've got a couple things in the boiling pot.'

Abraham: 'Right.'

Butera: 'Which are working.'

Abraham: 'Oh, good.'

utera: 'And we'll just have to put our heads together, see what we can come up with.

Abraham: 'Oh, that's wonderful. I need something.'

Butera: 'Ooh, I think you'll be impressed with what I'm doing.'

Abraham: 'Wonderful.'

Butera: '[Kumar] is in Singapore at the moment. I've got things happening.'

Abraham: 'Oh, that's good.'

On 28 July, Tony rang again, advising Butera that an Italian caterer wanted to 'buy in' on a future drug deal.

Butera: 'What's his terms and conditions?'

Tony: 'Ah, he just wants to buy half.'

Butera: 'How much for?'

Tony: 'Straight out two hundred.'

Butera: 'Thousand?'

Tony: 'Yeah.'

Butera: 'Really?'

Tony: 'No, I'm fair dinkum ... I just want to know if I'm a hundred per cent sure if you had it for what we agreed on.'

Butera: 'Well, why don't you wait ... I'll show you how serious I am. The only thing I haven't got in my favour is that my other man is not here. I've indicated to you he will be back here in the middle of August. All right, now yesterday something was supposed to happen which was adjourned. It's not, ah, going to be adjourned any further. On Monday, it happens or it doesn't happen, full stop.'

Tony: 'Right, well, I'm not waiting for that deal there to go through. I've been waiting for your mate to come back.'

Butera: 'Tony, listen, I've got enough money to buy in now on my own. Mate, I had, in two days, all right, I've had a hundred and fifty thousand dollars in my hands.'

A man called Pete then rang Butera about the Monday deal.

Pete: 'I spoke to Charlie.'

Butera: 'Yeah, is everything okay?'

Pete: 'He said that the small ones he can get them any time. But he, with the big ones, you'll have to talk to him.'

Butera: 'Well, hang on, what does he mean by small?'

Pete: 'You know, like thousand, two thousand dollar ones.'

Butera: 'Ah, jeez, mate, fuck, one thousand two thousand dollars, these guys fuckin' spend one thousand two thousand dollars going out to dinner. What are you doing to me?'

Tony: 'Those small ones he said he can get them seven days a week, right. But the big ones ... he'll have to ... see how their system works and how if it can be done. He'll let me know.'

Butera: 'Did you tell him it was for me?'

Tony: 'I said, no, Frank's doing me a favour. In the same way, he's gonna, sorta, like, you know, we'll compensate it, right, and he turned around, he said, no, I don't want anything. Gosh, if I can do him [Charlie] a favour, fuck, you know, I'll bend backwards for it.'

On 8 August, Larry rang saying a supply that was to have been available had been 'burnt' (seized by police).

Larry: 'It's fucking ... when I need something.'

Butera: 'No, it's a bugger of a thing, mate.'

Larry: 'Yeah, well, just all over Melbourne, mate, you know, it would be a perfect time for you to be flring. There's not a thing in Melbourne, mate.'

Butera: 'God, it's that dried up.'

It was the same story in a call to Butera from Rocky.

Rocky: 'Eh, things are too bad, mate.'

Butera: 'Yeah, that's what I have heard.'

Rocky: 'There is nothing, nothing. I'm losing a lot of fucking money. I've got people that are telephoning me from other places interstate and I can't get them anything.'

Butera: 'But listen to me, Rock, someone telephoned me last week, a friend of mine ... he has to bring me something then I will let you know.'

Rocky: 'We will sell it all, don't worry. If the stuff is really good, we will cut it and we will sell it in small quantities. Only like that we can make a bit.'

In another conversation, Rocky lamented that the shipment was not arriving sooner.

Rocky: 'If he would have fucking returned now, mate, we could make money by the spades full.'

Butera: 'You know, it's not as if it can't be sold, but the problem is that he isn't here. I don't have to explain the situation to you. You know how it is ... that is more dangerous than a bomb, mate.'

Rocky: 'When you can, you can. When you can't, you have to stop, no.'

Butera: 'Yeah, but slowly, slowly, Rock. I see it like this: if you walk slow, you walk secure, no?'

Rocky: 'Yeah, all right, mate.'

Butera: 'Well, Rock, we'll see. As soon as he arrives, I'll give you a telephone call.'

On August 14, a courier, Rayan Wanta Pinrenu, flew into Melbourne from Bangkok. Within days, he was joined by two others, Manjit Singh Namtanee and Gurdas Singh Narula, also from Bangkok. Narula then made a telephone call to Singapore. Soon after, Kuldip Kumar, brother of Butera's overseas contact and also once a partner in Delhi Express Travel in Melbourne, was recorded telephoning Butera to advise him that a shipment had already arrived safely in Melbourne, and that he was on his way to Melbourne to handle arrangements. Butera immediately telephoned a Melbourne contact, boasting: 'One of my people's arriving on Tuesday ... I'm looking forward to getting a Porsche, mate.'

Next, he rang Larry.

Butera: 'I've got someone flying in on Tuesday.'

Larry: 'Yeah?'

Butera: 'With something for you.'

Larry: 'Oh, lovely.'

On his arrival, Kumar booked into the Hilton Hotel, immediately rang Butera, and got a taxi to Butera's office. Two hours later, Butera phoned Larry: 'Everything's organised.'

Apart from further meetings with Kumar, at the Hilton, at his office in Reservoir and at his home at Glenroy, Butera was observed by undercover AFP officers going to a rendezvous. A car picked him up, drove off, then returned to Butera's parked car, where police watched him getting something from behind the front seat, he then return to the other car and drove off. Narula and Namtanee were arrested in a car in St Kilda, and Pinrenu was arrested in a room they shared at the nearby Kingsway Motel. Heroin weighing 660 grams (worth well over $1 million at street level prices) was recovered from a black briefcase, hidden inside a larger brown suitcase stashed in a wardrobe.

Caught red-handed, all three confessed, with Namtanee writing out a statement implicating Butera as the buyer prearranged in Singapore by Kumar. Arrested separately at the Hilton, Kumar acknowledged: 'I told them that Frank was my connection. He would help me get a connection. When, in fact, he, Frank, the lawyer, did not exist in all this.'

Kumar claimed he had been dealing with Butera only in relation to a legal matter resulting from the suspension nine months previously of Delhi Express Travel over the disappearance of international airline tickets. Likewise, when confronted by Sergeant William Taylor of the AFP, Butera claimed that Kumar had come all the way from Singapore to see him about the airline ticket affair, because he was upset after hearing that Butera had made a statement to another lawyer denouncing him and others as 'international crooks'. Told he had been nominated as the buyer for the seized heroin, Butera said: 'That's a lot of rubbish. He [Kumar] contacted me, but nothing, nothing in regard to drugs. I had nothing to do with it.'

What he did not know until he faced court was that the AFP knew exactly what he had had to do with it. Legal privilege could not protect him from a legal tap on his phone. In popular legal jargon, his pretence of a legal alibi to cover his illegal drug dealing was laughed out of court.

10

Lord Mayoral Embarrassment

Irvin Peter Rockman was known as a flashy, high-flying multi-millionaire, years before it became the fashion among leading entrepreneurs in the traditionally conservative Melbourne business community. An energetic ideas man, he shunned the staid image of a backroom money man in favour of the spotlight of publicity. Opening nights, charity bashes and celebrity functions were hardly complete without Rockman. Known as 'Rocky', he was Melbourne's Lord Mayor for two terms from 1977 to 1979 and was narrowly defeated when he stood for a third term. He was awarded the CBE for services to the city of Melbourne in the 1980 New Year's Honours list. He was on the council from 1973 until 1981.

He owns the luxurious 200-room Rockman's Regency Hotel in Lonsdale Street, which was completed in 1982 at a cost of $20 million. It was designed as a relatively small hotel, specialising in personalised service. It has proven to be a great success and attracts many national and international sporting and show business celebrities as regular guests.

Rockman has been involved in varied business activities, including wine shops, hotel-motels, finance companies, catering and property development. Rockman became an accomplished underwater photographer, pilot, windsurfer and diver. In his youth he was a fine athlete. Some of his underwater photographs were considered so good that they were exhibited and profits from their sale at one show were given to Odyssey House drug rehabilitation centre. Regularly listed in the top 200 wealthy people in the country, *Business Review Weekly* magazine estimated his wealth in 1990 to be more than $100 million.

It seemed to be a dream life. He was often mentioned as a possible State or federal parliamentarian and was an outspoken supporter of Melbourne, casinos and tourism to Victoria. A charming man, he had a wide range of friends and associates. One of them, the son of a retired NSW Supreme Court judge, Justice Ronald Cross, eventually turned things sour for the high flyer. Peter James Cross, former tuna fisherman, maths teacher, university student, drug smuggler and protected witness, was the man who dragged Irvin Rockman's name through the legal system in relation to cocaine.

Years earlier, Rockman had gone out of his way to deny any involvement with cocaine. He told veteran *Sun* reporter Tom Prior in 1983: 'As far as "coke" is concerned, there is no way you can take it and work as hard as I do. I'm nowhere as interesting as some of the stories you hear about me.'

Cross was a strange mix. He went to a Sydney grammar school and then did law for a year before quitting to take labouring jobs in Sydney and Melbourne. When he turned 19, Cross became a tuna fisherman and worked on both the eastern and southern coastlines of Australia. After four years he went to Melbourne University, lived in Carlton, married, had a son and completed a science degree. He joined the Education Department and was given a position as a maths teacher at Eltham High School, where he met an impressionable student named Cassandra Ogdon. The relationship would eventually cost the girl her life.

After his marriage broke up, Cross returned to tuna fishing before getting a teaching post at the Caulfield Institute of Technology. In 1980 he met a woman at a Carlton hotel, an English teacher at a Collingwood school. He later moved in with her. Through this woman, her architect brother and a Melbourne model, who was a friend of the group, Cross began to move up in the social world. He started to meet the rich and powerful. It was while living what he described as a 'trendy type of lifestyle' that he met Irvin Rockman. Cross loved his new lifestyle and became a regular at parties in South Yarra, Brighton and Toorak. Rockman was later to say that he found Cross to be 'well educated, articulate and humorous'. Cross said that it was around this time that he first tried cocaine and then began to use it about once a month.

In 1981 Cross was given a book to read. The book was to change his life. It was entitled *Snowblind* by Robert Sabbag, the story of Zachary Swan, a United States cocaine smuggler in the early 1970s. Cross saw this book as a revelation, a virtual do-it-yourself manual on how to smuggle cocaine. Swan was a person fascinated with maths, just like Cross. The Australian set out to emulate the activities of the book, even using similar smuggling techniques. He took to drug smuggling in a big way and later admitted to four importations of cocaine from South America between 1981 and 1984. But before he was to make his first trip to South America, during school holidays in 1981, he knew he needed a contact, someone who was living in a country where cocaine was available. Enter his former student, Cassandra Ogdon. Cassandra won a university exchange scholarship and spent 1981-82 in Bolivia. Cross found this out and duped Cassandra's mother into providing the address in Bolivia. Cross contacted the girl and later visited her in Cochabamba, the second biggest city in Bolivia. Eventually, after a little trial and error, Cross made his connection and began to bring cocaine back to Australia, first in small amounts. He alleged in his statement tendered at the inquiry that the first two shipments, in 1981 and 1982, which cost a total of $16,000, were financed by Rockman.

In a statement to investigators, Cross said that he wanted to go back to Bolivia to get more cocaine in 1983. He said he approached Rockman to finance the trip, but the businessman refused. Cross was well connected by this time. He had another powerful friend, but this one was way over the other side of the tracks – a notorious underworld hit man, Christopher Dale Flannery. Cross had met the killer through a mutual associate in Melbourne and they had hit it off. Cross would often have a few beers with Flannery at a hotel in Sydney near Mascot Airport. In 1983, Cross approached Flannery and asked him to finance a trip to Bolivia to import one kilogram of cocaine. He wanted $20,000, and Flannery came up with $18,000, saying the money was partly provided by two NSW police officers. Cross found the drugs more expensive than he imagined and had to settle for half a kilogram.

The drugs were sold to a Melbourne schoolteacher, a doctor and a real estate agent for a total of $64,000. After expenses, Cross and his financiers cleared $45,000. In September the following year Flannery again provided money, this time for an importation of about three kilos of cocaine. The hit man even provided a new contact in Bolivia to provide the cocaine. Flannery and Cross made about $170,000 each from the deal.

Those who know Cross say he was fascinated with the underworld and loved to be around a known killer like Flannery. It looked as though the two of them would continue in drug dealings for some years, but Flannery was killed on 9 May 1985 during a Sydney underworld war. This did not frighten Cross away from the heavy criminals. Indeed, the former schoolteacher and son of a senior judge vowed revenge for the death of his mate and on at least two occasions was involved in plots to murder the man he believed had ordered Flannery's death. Cross has admitted that twice he was with armed men who planned to kill Sydney gangster George Freeman, who they believed had organised Flannery's death. Twice they went to the Sydney suburb of Maroubra, to the doctor's surgery of Dr Nick Paltos, a man later convicted of serious drug offences.

Cross and his group knew that Freeman regularly went to Paltos's surgery. They planned to kill him outside the building. What they did not know was that Australian Federal Police were working on Paltos, and had the surgery under surveillance. When the would-be killers saw people near the surgery, they feared they were men who had been hired to protect Freeman. The murder attempts were called off. Freeman died in March 1990 from a heart attack during a severe asthma attack.

Cross continued his drug activities and moved further into the underworld after the failed murder bids. He took to carrying a handgun and handling vast amounts of cash. He was finally arrested by National Crime Authority investigators in a North Melbourne flat on 3 October 1986, during a $75,000 cocaine deal. It did not take long for him to agree to tell all, plead guilty and finally to cooperate as a protected 'supergrass' police witness. Cross was sentenced to four years' jail in December 1986, but within six months he was out of jail and in the care of the Australian Federal Police Witness Protection Scheme.

At his trial, Justice Nicholson said: 'I have little doubt that this cooperation has placed your life in serious danger.' Cross was moved interstate under an alias as fears grew for his life. He was the star witness in a trial that resulted in three major drug figures being convicted on marijuana and cocaine charges. One of the men was the notorious Dennis William 'Fat Cat' Smith, a Bendigo-born criminal who built a vice and drug empire in Manila. Cross's evidence played a crucial part in Smith receiving 11 years in jail, with a minimum of nine, over the drug charges in the Melbourne County Court in November 1989. Two others were also convicted: Kerry Joseph Ashford was sentenced to 10 years with a minimum of eight and Thomas Schevella was sentenced to eight years with a minimum of six.

When Cross decided to cooperate with the National Crime Authority, he talked about his dealings, not only with the underworld, but also with some of Melbourne's socialites. Shortly after his arrest, he told surprised investigators about his relationship with Rockman and talked of sharing cocaine with Rockman and others at the businessman's Gembrook farm. The NCA had the brief to investigate the Sydney underworld murders, including that of Flannery's, through a special operation code-named 'Curtains'. It was through Cross's connection with the hit man that the NCA was able to investigate further claims, including those made against Rockman.

Even though there was no suggestion that Rockman was connected with Flannery, the underworld or murders, Cross was the link that enabled the NCA to enlarge the investigation under the 'Curtains' probe. One obvious area the NCA needed to check was Cross's claim that he had tried to enlist Cassandra Ogdon in Bolivia. Investigators approached her in January 1987 and she said she suspected, but had no direct knowledge, that Cross was smuggling drugs. She was one of more than 30 witnesses interviewed and considered to be one of the least important. Later in the year, investigators decided to review the case and call witnesses to give sworn evidence in secret sessions of the NCA. On 5 July 1987, Cassandra was issued with an NCA subpoena under the specific reference of Operation Curtains. She would have seen on the paperwork that the broad investigation related to the underworld and a series of murders. There is evidence to suggest that because of what she read on the subpoena, she jumped to the conclusion that her life was in danger.

On 17 August 1987, Cassandra Ogdon killed herself, only hours before she was to give evidence before the NCA. She suffocated herself by putting two plastic bags over her head while in the bedroom of her rented Brunswick Street, Fitzroy, house. There is evidence that three attempts were made to intimidate her before she was due to give evidence. A live bullet was left at her mother's home on a night in May 1987. In early August, two men questioned her at her work in Richmond about what she had said in her original statement to the NCA. Three days before she was to attend the secret session of the NCA, she said she received a phone call at home warning her not to give evidence. She did not tell police about any of the threats.

When she decided to take her own life, she wrote a long note detailing a series of allegations about cocaine use. The letter, admitted as evidence in May 1988 at a coronial inquest into her death, named Rockman in connection with cocaine. The note said she had attended a party with Cross in Malvern that was also attended by Rockman and another woman.

'We ate dinner, had coke. I watched them gloat like smug little kids, I had huge fear instilled into me that night,' the note read. It went on: 'I do not prefer to wait for the day that the NCA squeeze me to the point of necessitating my murder at the hands of hoons of Melbourne's leading business tycoons. I can comfortably take my own life, and eliminate my case for fear rather more quickly than they have promised to do to me if I "crack in court".'

The letter said that she was surprised when Cross arrived to see her in Bolivia. 'He arrived with no contacts, two weeks with which to organise himself, and a pile of money supplied to him by his friend Irvin Rockman.' A statement from Cross was read to the inquest, but the former schoolteacher refused to confirm or deny it from the witness box. In the signed statement, he spoke of the first trip to Bolivia in 1981. 'I divulged my plans to a friend of mine at that time, Irvin Rockman. He inquired of me as to how risky my plan was. I indicated that I was prepared to give it a go and he agreed to finance the deal.'

He said that when the cocaine arrived, 'the ceremonial opening of the package took place in Gembrook at Irvin Rockman's farm. Irvin was present with myself and others, not including Cassie.' Rockman gave evidence at the coronial inquest. On oath he said: 'In answer to the question, "Was I involved with Peter Cross in the plan to import cocaine to Australia", I state that I was not so involved.' He added: 'I have never been involved with Peter Cross nor any other person in a plan to import cocaine, any drug or anything else from Bolivia to Australia.' He also denied making any threats or warnings to Ogdon. Rockman refused to answer a number of questions relating to cocaine use on the grounds of self-incrimination. He refused to answer questions including whether he had ever taken cocaine, whether he had ever had cocaine in his possession, whether he had given Cross money for cocaine. He also refused to say whether he had seen Cross with cocaine at his (Rockman's) Gembrook farm. He said that Cross had been to the farm several times.

Rockman said that in 1984 he had given Cross a personal loan of $16,000 to buy a flat. He said the money had been given and repaid by cheque. Rockman also denied any recollection of being present with Cross and Ogdon at a party in Malvern. The coroner, Hal Hallenstein, found that Rockman was present at the Malvern house with Cassandra Ogdon and Cross, 'in circumstances where cocaine was present and used'. He found that, before her death, Ogdon 'reasonably believed' Rockman was involved in the importation of cocaine with Cross and 'that the need for her silence had been specifically and unequivocally demanded' at the Malvern cocaine party. After the inquest, counsel representing Rockman said: 'Clearly he has been exonerated.'

In August 1987, National Crime Authority officers raided several properties owned by Rockman. Later that year, a case prepared against the former Lord Mayor collapsed when the then Federal Director of Public Prosecutions, Ian Temby, QC, refused to indemnify Cross to give evidence.

As published in the *Sun*, Temby rejected an NCA request for the Cross indemnity because no allegations were made that Rockman was involved in a commercial enterprise – he did not sell cocaine and because Cross himself linked up with an underworld figure to import cocaine valued at $400,000. While Rockman's alleged activities did not reflect credit on him, if he were required to go before a jury Rockman's good service to the community would make a conviction less likely. It was also stated that the NCA and DPP could be criticised for using a disreputable figure to get the scalp of a prominent figure. It was distasteful to launch a prosecution purely because the person was prominent, like using a 'shark, not just a mackerel, to catch a spratt', the DPP advice said. 'The conviction of Rockman is possible, but by no means certain.'

The case against Rockman is dead – and so is Cassie Ogdon, the former exchange student pulled into the whole dirty business because she had the misfortune to be taught maths by a man who wanted to be a coke smuggler. Cassie became a frightened woman who took her life rather than testify on matters that now, in the eyes of the law, no longer even matter.

11
Nunawading Affair

Since 11 November 1975, governments, particularly Labor ones, have viewed hostile upper houses of Parliament with varying degrees of suspicion and paranoia. It was then that the sacking of the Whitlam Labor Government by the Governor-General, Sir John Kerr, after the conservative-dominated Senate deferred Supply, effectively destroyed a democratically-elected Government. Ever since then, the once passive concept of upper houses as gentlemen's clubs has been banished forever.

In Victoria, the fear of a hostile upper house goes back much further, right back to 1947 when John Cain senior's Labor Government was brought down when Supply was blocked by the Legislative Council. A conservative-controlled upper house has been seen as an ongoing threat by all Victorian Labor stalwarts.

In March 1985, after three years in power, John Cain senior's son had the chance to create history, to be the first Labor Government to win consecutive elections in Victoria. Facing re-election, and on a popular wave, he was confident of winning a majority in both houses. Cain campaigned on the basis of 'honesty, integrity and reality', and largely on his Government's record over the previous three years. The 2 March election did create history. The ALP was re-elected with a reduced majority in the lower house, but Cain confidently predicted Labor would finally control the upper house.

One of the upper house seats expected to go to Labor was getting closer and closer as each crucial vote was counted. The seat, which was to haunt the ALP for years, was Nunawading. On the first count, ALP candidate Bob Ives beat Liberal Rosemary Varty by 38 votes. On a recount, it was a tie at 54,821 votes each. In a quite extraordinary event, the returning officer, Kathleen Leonard, decided to draw one of the candidates' names from a ballot box to break the deadlock. The name was Bob Ives and victory was declared to the ALP, giving it a 23-21 majority in the upper house.

The Liberal Party was not impressed and appealed to the Court of Disputed Returns, headed by Supreme Court judge Justice Starke. During a three-week hearing, ALP state secretary Peter Batchelor could sometimes be seen sitting behind the party's counsel, Peter Black, QC, taking great interest in the proceedings. On 8 July, Justice Starke ruled that at least 36 votes had been wrongly excluded by polling clerk errors from the count and recount, and he ordered a new election.

Both parties said they were confident and went into the Nunawading rerun on 17 August with the same candidates. The ALP had to fight the normal swing against governments in a by-election and threw enormous resources into the campaign. The campaign was slick. In the week before the election, it looked a neck-and-neck race. A *Herald* poll conducted days before the election indicated that 15 per cent of voters would vote for minor parties and suggested that the result would rest on the distribution of preferences.

A Liberal party survey showed that the preferences from the Nuclear Disarmament Party, the DLP, the Call to Australia Party, the Democrats and the three Independents could hold the key. In a surprise move, the NDP decided not to direct preferences on their how-to-vote card. Previously, it had directed preferences to the Australian Democrats or the

ALP. This was a major blow to the ALP, which expected nearly all the NDP votes to flow to it through preferences. The NDP decision would split the preferences and cost the ALP anything up to 1500 votes, enough, some thought, to tip the balance to the Liberals.

A political plot was hatched, which was misleading, to say the least; a plot that would forever bury the image of the Cain Government as being 'squeaky clean'. A Melbourne solicitor, Nick Nikolaidou, authorised 120,000 Nuclear Disarmament how-to-vote cards that ultimately favoured the ALP in preferences, contrary to the official NDP cards. The $800 payment for the new cards was underwritten by Peter Batchelor.

Batchelor received legal advice that the new cards were legal before he embarked on a course of action which, it was later argued, misled voters at the election. A day before the election, the new tickets were picked up from a city printer and taken to the ALP's Ringwood office. On the morning of the election, members and supporters of the ALP met at the office for a final pep talk and briefing. It was at that meeting that some volunteers were asked to hand out the 'bogus' Nuclear Disarmament ticket rather than official ALP how-to-vote cards.

The ALP supporters were taken to the 52 polling booths to distribute cards. Some handed out Labor cards, others handed out the unsourced nuclear cards. The NDP later claimed that some of its supporters were duped into believing that the official non-preference cards had been replaced by the new cards, which supported Labor on preferences. The NDP claimed some of its people ended up handing out the Labor connected cards, believing they were last-minute replacements for the NDP.

Ironically, in the days before the election while the last details of the plot were being completed, Batchelor was prepared to take the high moral ground on how elections should be fought. 'We are too busy campaigning in Nunawading to worry about dirty tricks,' he told the *Sun*. Dirty tricks or not, the plot failed and Liberal candidate Varty was comfortably elected to the upper house. The NDP candidate, Jenny Cotterell, received about 2.4 per cent – 2530 votes.

In the election aftermath, Batchelor denied that the ALP was connected with the 'alternative' Nuclear Disarmament card – not once, but three times. He told Channel 10 reporter Jane Phelan, *Herald* journalist Shane Green and NDP convener Martin Peake on separate occasions that there was no ALP involvement. He tried to blame Monash University students for the cards. He claimed false allegation of ALP involvement was started on polling day by the Liberals. 'It had nothing to do with us,' he said.

Three days after the election, Martin Peake complained to the Chief Electoral Officer, Mr Richardson, about the cards, and an investigation was launched to see if the matter was a breach of the Act. Richardson called the police into the investigation and a slow fire was started that took more than a month to take hold. The coals still burn. In late September it became public that police were interviewing some key ALP people in connection with the cards. Detectives had found voters who said they had been misled by the scheme. On 27 September, the *Sun* published a front-page report headed: LABOR LINKED TO FRAUD POLL. It stated that there could have been a 'Watergate-type conspiracy to fix the recent Nunawading election'.

The matter then slowly began to open up. It leaked out that some key Labor people were refusing to cooperate with police. Lists were freely bandied about claiming to show who was involved. Many were full of misinformation put about by political factions. On 4 October, the *Sun* identified Batchelor as a key figure in the distribution of the cards. It became clear in Labor circles that this was not an issue that could be 'toughed out' in the hope it would go away. On 9 October, Batchelor released a statement admitting that he and other ALP figures were involved in the matter.

He claimed that he had said the ALP was not involved because he had helped organise the cards as a private citizen rather than the State secretary of the party. He said it was not an authorised party action. It didn't wash with anyone. State political reporters, most who apparently had seen so many political dirty tricks that they did not seem overly concerned with Nunawading, finally seemed to sense a scandal and descended on the ALP's offices in Carlton to confront Batchelor. He held a conference where he read a prepared statement and then refused to answer questions yelled to him by the pack. It was a shambles.

The parliamentary press pack, by now almost baying for political blood, headed for Spring Street, to take on Labor Premier John Cain. They were all there ready to crack the Premier. A calm Premier used the frenzy to ensure that no serious line of questioning ever developed. It was a case of which reporter had the loudest voice, each one seemingly trying to outdo the others. John Cain was more than a match. He took them on for more than an hour and they left knowing no more than when they got there.

Away from the grandstanding, the police investigation ground on, despite the lack of cooperation by some key figures. An Upper House Parliamentary Select Committee was later told that the police inquiry resulted in recommendations that 10 people be charged over the cards, including Batchelor; Michael Salvaris, a former adviser to the Premier; solicitor Nick Nikolaidou; and a senior official in the Premier's Department, Ian Baker, since elected to Parliament and promoted to Minister for Agriculture.

One of the police who handled the investigation, Detective Sergeant Denny Van Maanenberg, told the committee

Batchelor was less than open to police and had misled investigators. In their report, police suggested a judicial inquiry might be the only way to get to the bottom of the matter.

The political stunt that Batchelor explained away to the *Age* in these terms, 'I don't describe it as dirty tricks, more like hard politics', just refused to lie down. After all, there had been an official complaint, a police investigation, and Chief Electoral Officer Richardson had to make a decision as to whether anyone should be prosecuted. When the more than 300-page police report was finished, legal advice was called upon to see if charges should be laid.

In total, a phenomenal nine legal opinions were received. One said there was no case and another said while there may be a case, discretion could be used not to prosecute. The rest said there was a case. On 17 March 1986, the Director of Public Prosecutions, John Coldrey, QC, found a prima facie case against 11 people, including Batchelor, Salvaris and Nikolaidou. With the status of a Supreme Court judge, the DPP is supposed to have the final say on whether prosecutions should be launched.

The Government maintained that it would not interfere with Richardson's decision whether to prosecute or not. Yet, after the DPP's advice was received, Richardson's public service boss, the Director-General of the Property and Services Department, Bill Russell, suggested to Richardson that he should get another legal opinion from the Solicitor-General, Hartog Berkeley, QC. Richardson later said he believed the suggestion to seek the advice had been instigated by the then minister, Andrew McCutcheon. This was later denied by both Russell and McCutcheon.

Nevertheless, Richardson sought the advice from Berkeley, believing that was what his minister wanted him to do. The advice came back that there was no evidence to support prosecution. Subsequent advice from Coldrey, backed by

Senior Crown Prosecutor John Morrissey, QC, rejected the Solicitor-General's advice. Another opinion by Melbourne lawyer David Habersberger, a man who had represented Richardson previously, also dismissed the Berkeley advice.

With this weight of conflicting advice, Richardson had to make a decision on whether to prosecute, an action that would have damaged the Labor Government. A file note, later released after a Freedom of Information court case, showed that on 7 May 1986 Berkeley contacted the Assistant Crown Solicitor, Alistair Mclean, and said the Government would prefer that no charges be laid that week.

The day before, the Government had been put under great pressure in Parliament with the Opposition concentrating on the Nunawading issue and producing confidential police information about the investigation. But Parliament was due to rise on 8 May and John Cain was also due to travel overseas the following week for a fortnight, well away from any local controversy. It did not matter. On 8 May, Richardson made a public statement that he did not intend to prosecute anyone, saying he 'attached particular importance to the views set out in the joint advice of the Solicitor-General and junior counsel'. He did not mention that he received subsequent legal opinions, including one from the DPP, rejecting the Solicitor-General's view.

When documents were released through the Administrative Appeals Tribunal, after an FOI appeal by journalist Paul Chadwick and the *Sun* in June 1987, the issue was back on the political agenda. The Government fought the FOI case. In May 1986 Cain said it would be 'completely wrong' to release the legal opinions on the case. However, by June the following year, after the Government lost the case, he said, 'I would prefer them to be made public'.

Berkeley's 'request' to Mclean that no charges be laid on the week that Parliament was sitting created the suggestion that there was political meddling behind the scenes with the alleged independence of the Chief Electoral Officer.

Berkeley wrote a letter explaining that it was his 'perceptions' that the Government would not want charges laid that week. He said he had not been told of any Government preferences on the timing of any charges. He was not prepared to enlarge on his views. In a quite extraordinary outburst outside the High Court in Canberra on 11 June, Berkeley told respected senior Channel 10 journalist Elissa O'Neil he would not be cross-examined in the street and threatened to 'kick those blokes' balls in', referring to the camera crew.

The Government had maintained all along that Richardson would act independently. The judge at the Administrative Appeals Tribunal who heard the FOI case, Judge Rowlands, said in his decision, 'The independence of which the Chief Electoral Officer spoke does not sit comfortably with the fact that he passed on earlier opinions to his departmental head who consulted the minister before offering unsolicited advice to him, upon which he acted'. But the statute of limitations had long passed and the issue became political rather than legal. No prosecutions could be launched a year after the incidents.

While Nikolaidou resigned from the law firm where he worked, Batchelor refused to quit as State Secretary of the Labor Party. Cain said: 'I've got the greatest confidence in him.' Not only did Batchelor survive, but also he prospered. In early 1990 he surfaced again, this time as the endorsed candidate for the safer-than-safe Labor stronghold of Thomastown. The man who allegedly misled voters, police, the media, the NDP, and was fortunate not to have been charged, was set for a new career as a politician. In 1988, the Labor Party had polled 72.4 per cent of the vote in the second safest seat in the State, but Batchelor lost a huge 24 per cent in a by-election for the seat on 3 February 1990.

The Opposition Leader, Alan Brown, declared of the result: 'One can only say that this is the beginning of the end for the Cain Labor Government in Victoria. It is also the end for John Cain as leader of of the Labor Party in this State and he should now seriously consider his position.' Political rhetoric is cheap, but on 7 August that year, then in the midst of further troubles, John Cain, the longest-serving Victorian Labor Premier, stood down.

12

Continental Scandal

It all began as a straightforward fraud squad investigation. It ended with one man dead and a senior policeman professionally destroyed. In 1985, a fraud squad investigation snowballed into a major probe into police accepting discount airline fares to travel overseas. The inquiry, which lasted 14 months, resulted in damage to the reputations of both the Victoria Police Force and the Cain Government. Most importantly, it questioned the very integrity of so-called independent police investigations.

The situation became such a political minefield that the policeman who headed the inquiry, Chief Inspector Max Castree, disowned his own report because of what he believed was outrageous outside interference. In April 1985, police raided an office where Christopher Sundt Brading was using a fake airline company to organise cheap airline tickets. The deal was simple: his fake company would get cheap 'industry price' tickets on the premise that the people who bought them were employed in the industry. Brading's name had figured in investigations by the Costigan commission into international arms dealing and links with the notorious Nugan Hand Bank. When police raided the office, they found paperwork connecting Brading to a high-level Continental Airlines executive, Robert Tanfield.

The name soon rang a bell with the police command because Tanfield was a close friend of Assistant Commissioner Bob Stewart and was a regular guest at private police functions. Raids on Tanfield's city office found paperwork showing that many senior police had travelled on cut price air tickets under false occupations. Tanfield was charged with 32 counts of fraud, and Stewart, on holiday in London, was ordered to return immediately. He went straight to police headquarters where he was interviewed and charged on 8 August 1985 with forgery and conspiracy. Four days later, he took early retirement.

On 17 August, the *Age* broke the story that up to 20 senior police were under investigation over the cheap tickets saga. It was one of the few times in more than a decade under Chief Commissioner Mick Miller that there was a hint of scandal about the force. On 4 September, the *Herald* revealed that the Cain Government had appointed a legal task force under Leonard Flanagan, QC, to oversee the police investigation.

The investigation became bogged down and side-tracked on matters that were not related to possible criminal charges of police, or anyone else involved in the cheap ticket scam. The investigators and the lawyers did not get on, and pulled in different directions. In the end, they hardly spoke to each other; it was a shambles. The investigation was taken over by Robert Redlich, QC, and his report recommended a board of inquiry into the affair. Miller opposed it and Cabinet backed him.

On 9 October 1985, Miller wrote to the *Herald* and said there was no need for a public inquiry. He said that police anticipated that many people, 'perhaps hundreds', would be charged as part of the investigation. About two weeks earlier, the *Sun* published news that the task force was going to check all MPs, judges and magistrates to see if they had taken cheap Continental flights, a story that was repeated in the *Age* on 31 May the following year.

At the time, the then head of police internal investigations, Assistant Commissioner Kel Glare, later promoted to Chief

Commissioner, said he believed the probe would take two years.

Later, before the Administrative Appeals Tribunal, Glare said that he understood that the then Police Minister, Race Mathews, advised senior police to hand briefs of evidence to the Director of Public Prosecutions, John Coldrey, QC, setting a two-week deadline in November 1985. Glare described the time frame as 'unrealistic'. Mathews later said he did not interfere in the probe and that it was wrong to say it was curtailed.

In his report the head of the task force, Chief Inspector Castree wrote: 'The setting of such a time limit is conducive to a less than thorough or adequate investigation being undertaken. I do not accept responsibility for the thoroughness or otherwise of the investigators as these matters are now clearly beyond my control.'

Briefs of evidence on 15 police, two public servants and 18 members of the public were handed to the DPP. For one man, the waiting and the pressure became too much. The former airline executive, the former friend and confidant of senior police, Robert Tanfield, could stand it no more. Tanfield was found dead in his car on 7 February 1986, at his Maryborough property. He committed suicide by breathing exhaust gases from his car. The task force later wrote that Tanfield was distraught about being charged and was heading towards alcoholism. 'Although working, his financial position was in ruins and he felt an outcast [from] and humiliated [by] the people he considered his friends, the police.'

To the end, Tanfield maintained he had done nothing wrong in getting police contacts cheap flights on planes. He could get police trips to New Zealand for $50 return. He said that it was better for business to have 'bums on seats' than half-empty planes. Tanfield was a man who collected police-related objects such as diaries, tie pins and cuff links. He was a member of the Police Association Club and worked out at the police gym. He was a police groupie.

In October 1986, the DPP returned his advice on the police briefs and concluded that no one should be charged over the investigation. On 16 October, charges already instituted against former Bob Stewart and a travel agent were dropped on the advice of the DPP. The police task force, which had worked for 14 months on the Continental probe, was far from happy. In a report, the task force had recommended charges against seven serving police and two retired policemen. Their recommendations were ignored. The report, which was leaked to the *Sun* in March 1987, recommended charges against a high-ranking officer, a retired assistant commissioner, a superintendent, chief inspector, sergeant, senior constable, retired senior constable, and a constable. It found that some of the police investigated had signed false declarations that they were airline employees. The task force found that other police did not know that documents had been forged for them without their knowledge. Senior police were furious that the report was made public. A high-ranking policeman was assigned to investigate the leak into the Continental inquiry.

Those who travelled under the scheme run by Tanfield were given a discount through an interline travel agreement for airline employees. Others were given discounts because they were supposedly in the travel industry. The report slammed the honesty of some police interviewed, accusing some of unacceptable behaviour and others of lying to investigators. Glare later said that six officers were privately disciplined for their 'indiscretions'.

After the story in the *Sun*, Cain strongly supported the decision not to prosecute in the face of the police advice. He said it was right and proper that the recommendations of the DPP should be followed. It was not a view he would make public when the same DPP found that there was a case to answer against 11 people, including several linked with the ALP, over the Nunawading how-to-vote card scandal.

The Continental probe sifted through 21,000 documents, interviewed 235 people and took 137 statements. More than 10,000 names were checked on computer and 31 serving or retired police were interviewed. Both the *Age* and *Herald* called for independent inquiries into the saga. Some police argued that the accepting of cheap tickets was not an offence because it was a common practice. They said that the offer was from a senior airline executive and that there was no intention to defraud anyone. The signing of a false statement of occupation was only a way of getting around a 'loophole'. Others argued that if anyone deliberately put a false occupation to paper in a bid to get a cheap flight then they were dangerously close to being on the wrong side of the law.

Some perceived subsequently that there was no judicial inquiry into the Continental scandal because the Government would then have been under great pressure to have a similar open inquiry into the Nunawading affair – an inquiry that would have damaged the ALP. No direct evidence has been unearthed to support the theory, but no one was prosecuted over Continental and no one was prosecuted over Nunawading.

13

Departure of a Governor

In late September 1985, the Prime Minister, Bob Hawke, while officially touring Queensland, told two political journalists in his entourage that 'a big story' was about to break in Victoria. Journalists become excited at the slightest hint of a breaking story. However, nothing would have titillated the two reporters more than an allusion by the Prime Minister to a possible political crisis in the sober, 'squeaky-clean' Victoria of the then Premier, John Cain. Naturally, the journalists pushed, but Hawke would not elaborate.

Only about 10 days later, after what was certainly a deliberate hint by a Prime Minister not known for faux pas, it was clear what Hawke had been anticipating. On 3 October, the Governor of Victoria, Rear Admiral Sir Brian Murray, made the unprecedented step of resigning his post over his acceptance of free overseas airline tickets. On the surface, Hawke's apparent knowledge of Sir Brian's imminent resignation seemed innocuous enough.

In the context of a storm that was already brewing in Victoria, it only added to the murkiness that still shrouds one of the biggest scandals of the 1980s, in which senior Victorian police and politicians, a major American airline and one of Victoria's most prominent entrepreneurs were implicated.

During the week beginning Monday 12 August 1985, the Premier had an urgent meeting with the Minister for Police and Emergency Services, Race Mathews, and Victoria's Chief Commissioner of Police, Mick Miller. John Cain was told that up to 20 of Victoria's most senior police had taken heavily discounted, or free, air tickets by posing as airline employees. The name of the airline was not mentioned at that stage. During the meeting, Miller argued against a judicial inquiry because of the blow it might strike to the morale of his force. The public perception of Victorian police, esteemed in comparison to other States, would also be jeopardised by a Royal Commission or similar wide-reaching judicial inquiry.

So, on Saturday 17 August, Cain announced that a 'proper and adequate' investigation into the ticket scandal would be conducted by the police themselves. The investigation would be aided by a legal task force headed by Victoria's Crown Counsel, Leonard Flanagan, QC. Exactly a week later, on 24 August, the Governor was unwittingly caught up when he and his wife flew out of Australia for an overseas holiday – the flight courtesy of Continental Airlines.

On 4 September, the *Herald* had revealed that police had interviewed the Minister for Transport, Tom Roper, over a letter he had written to an unnamed airline about preferred travel. Roper was quickly cleared by Cain of any ministerial impropriety, while investigations continued into allegations that senior public servants and office holders might be among the prominent figures who had accepted free or cheap air tickets. There is little doubt that at the time, like most people, Sir Brian and Lady Murray did not know which airline was being investigated. However, in the climate of suspicion sparked by the investigation, all the signs showed that never had there been a less prudent time for someone in Sir Brian's position to accept free travel from any airline.

It was obvious, however, that the decision to accept free tickets for an 'inaugural' Continental Airlines flight between London and Houston by Sir Brian and his wife was not made in haste. The circumstances under which the offer was made and accepted, five months earlier, would later add to evidence of sharp differences between Sir Brian – appointed to the office of Governor by a Liberal Premier, Lindsay Thompson, in 1982 – and John Cain. Relations between Sir Brian and Cain started to crumble soon after the Labor Government came to power in the same year, and before long not even the convention surrounding the confidentiality of their dealings could hide their differences. Such differences would ultimately give credence to suggestions that Sir Brian had been pressured into retiring by more than just the ticket affair.

Well before Sir Brian accepted the tickets, ties between Government House and the Premier had become icy and aloof. As early as 1982, journalists and political observers had little doubt that Cain would take the first opportunity to replace the former naval officer who had become Governor. Several much-publicised incidents seemed to confirm the rift between Spring Street and Government House.

In February 1985, Cain said he had 'spoken to' Lady Murray about a speech she had given, in which she said that Government House was cold in winter and was overdue for refurbishing. 'All I was concerned about was she mentioned matters that concerned Government in a situation which was not appropriate,' Cain insisted. He said he spoke to Lady Murray about 'a number of things' and that he had 'made clear what the role' of the Governor should be.

It was not the first time politics had intruded on the life of Sir Brian. In late 1984, he had taken the unprecedented step of going public to refute an Opposition claim that the Cain Government was threatening the future of the office of Governor. The Opposition, led by Jeff Kennett, had said that the Cain Government had already subjected the office of Governor to unprecedented humiliation and interference. Nonetheless, Cain was reportedly upset with the fact that Sir Brian had gone public on what he saw as a political matter.

In early February 1984, 600 millionaires from throughout

the world – members of the exclusive Young Presidents' Organisation – met for a world conference in Melbourne. Only those who had, by the age of 40, become chief executives of companies employing at least 50 people and turning over at least $5 million a year were at the time eligible for the ranks of the YPO.

Sir Brian enthusiastically welcomed the Young Presidents to Victoria. He even hosted a dinner for them at Government House. Among the millionaires at the conference were the chairman of Continental Airlines, Frank Lorenzo, who had flown in from Texas; and the Melbourne trucking magnate, Lindsay Fox. Notably absent from the festivities was Cain, who had refused to make a fuss about the arrival in Melbourne of the young presidents. Fox later publicly criticised Cain for not attending any YPO functions – a rebuke the Premier was said to deeply resent. The conference proved a boon for Fox, who nine months later was appointed by Lorenzo as chairman of a new international advisory board for Continental Airlines.

But the conference was the beginning of the end for Sir Brian. Fifteen months later, in May 1985, he accepted from Lorenzo free seats aboard an inaugural Continental flight for the forthcoming September. Convention required a Governor to tell the Premier if he was planning to leave the State. The Governor told Cain of his plans to leave for the Continental flight when they met at a function on 2 August – three weeks before Sir Brian and Lady Murray were due to leave. Cain was to say later that, at the time, he was unaware of any investigation into Continental Airlines and that Sir Brian had not said on which airline he was travelling. However, throughout the scandal, Cain maintained that he had cautioned Sir Brian about accepting free travel and advised him of the code of conduct preventing his ministers from accepting 'gifts'. The Governor obviously thought the code of conduct for government ministers did not apply to him.

On Tuesday 17 September – a few days before the Murrays returned from their trip – it was known that Continental Airlines was the unnamed airline involved in investigations. Cain then found out that the Governor was travelling with Continental Airlines. In fact, he was told that Sir Brian and Lady Murray had travelled from Australia to London via the United States, on free tickets.

The Murrays had also stopped over in France, Germany, Italy, Switzerland and England, staying in luxury accommodation. Their first stop was at Honolulu, where they stayed at Lindsay Fox's private villa for three days. Fox later joined them in Europe and they spent three days cruising the Mediterranean on a boat owned by a friend of Fox's. It was known that Fox, through Lorenzo, had arranged the free flight. Sir Brian later said that he believed he travelled to London from Sydney on tickets paid for by Continental Airlines, and that a flight from Frankfurt to Melbourne on Cathay Pacific was funded by reciprocal arrangements between the airlines. He was also believed to have told Cain that other flights in Europe were paid for by Fox.

However, under the safety of parliamentary privilege, Cain claimed the hospitality ran into 'much, much more' than just the flights. He refused to elaborate, but it was clear he was pointing the finger at Fox. Fox, himself a knockabout former truckie, told reporters seeking more information to 'get stuffed'. On 20 September, the day the Murrays arrived back in Melbourne, Cain immediately called on the Governor, demanding to know more details about their travel. A nonplussed Sir Brian argued that he could not see any relationship between his acceptance of courtesy free tickets and what the police inquiry was about: that police had signed documents claiming to be Continental employees before taking free or discounted flights.

The Cain–Murray confrontation at that time was all secret, in accordance with protocol for dealings between Premiers and Governors. Four days later, when Cain announced the appointment of a Queen's Counsel, Robert Redlich, to join a task force helping the police investigation into the police ticket rort, it was disclosed that all State MPs, judges, magistrates and police who had served in the previous five years would have their names checked against Continental's booking lists. No mention was made of the Governor. That same day, Bruce Guthrie at the *Herald* was told of the Governor's involvement by an anonymous caller. Guthrie was adamant the tip-off didn't come from the Government or the police.

While the *Herald* and suddenly other media sought confirmation, Sir Brian – aware that the story was about to break – issued a statement admitting he had accepted the free inaugural flight from Continental Airlines. He claimed this was 'in accordance with what the Governor understands to be customary practice in the airline industry'.

The next day, 3 October, a barrage of television cameras, press photographers and reporters followed an even-tempered Sir Brian and Lady Murray on a 'regular country tour' to Cobram, 235 kilometres from Melbourne. That morning, an *Age* editorial suggested that the issue posed a dilemma for Sir Brian, 'less one of legality than of propriety'. Although the editorial acknowledged that there was no evidence that the airline sought favours in return from the Governor or any other recipients of discounted or free tickets, 'Like Caesar's wife, the Queen's representative must be, and be seen to be, above any suspicion of being compromised or open to influence by providers of largesse'.

While Sir Brian toured Cobram his fate was sealed when the first edition of the *Herald* was placed on the Premier's desk. In a page-one story, it disclosed the existence of a forgotten colonial regulation barring Governors and their families from accepting free travel. Not even Cain had been aware of it. The colonial regulations specified, in part: 'Governors and their families are prohibited from receiving valuable presents ... whether in the shape of money, goods, free passages ...'. At 8.30 that night, Cain had a six-minute meeting with Sir Brian at Government House on his return from the country. Sir Brian baulked, telling Cain he would seek legal counsel.

Outside, Cain told the waiting media that the Governor had said he also wished to speak to the Liberal Opposition leader, Jeff Kennett, and National Party leader, Peter Ross-Edwards. It was later found, however, that this message had been confused: Sir Brian had not asked to see the leaders of the conservative parties – on the contrary, they had requested an audience with him, although Cain continued to contest this point. While Cain was speaking to the press, Sir Brian summoned his legal adviser, John Winneke, QC, himself the son of a former Victorian Governor, Sir Henry Winneke. At a subsequent meeting later that night between Cain and Sir Brian it was agreed that the Governor would resign. After meeting again with Sir Brian the next morning, the Premier attended Parliament for an hour, then went back to Government House for another meeting that lasted six hours, during which a financial settlement for Sir Brian was thrashed out. Late that night, Cain told a silent Parliament that Sir Brian had tendered his resignation as Governor of Victoria.

A short statement was read by the Premier, on behalf of Sir Brian. The statement said Sir Brian's 'overriding concern is, and always has been, to preserve the integrity of the Office of Governor'. It added: 'I would never wish to do anything that might or could be said to compromise the office and it is my hope that no one else in the community would ever wish by their words or actions to do otherwise.' In the ensuing debate, Cain denied that he had 'set a trap' for Sir Brian or that he had run a 'vendetta' against the Governor.

Kennett claimed that Sir Brian had been set up in what he termed a 'grubby affair'. By not ordering Sir Brian not to reject the air tickets, when he was first told about the travel, Cain had set a trap that was sprung on the Governor as soon as he returned. 'If I had wanted to remove him,' responded Cain, 'I could have done it any day during the past three and a half years. The Office of Governor is in my gift.'

By law, Cain was not required to grant Sir Brian a pension, nor was the Governor entitled to one under the Constitution Act until he had served a full five-year term. Yet, to see him go, he was prepared to grant Sir Brian a pension of $58,000 a year, a lump sum of $30,000, plus resettlement costs of up to $15,000, as well the use of a car for official business and a secretarial service for three months. The Opposition later claimed that Sir Brian and Lady Murray were forced to enter a written agreement gagging them from public comment about the affair, in exchange for the retirement package. Kennett said that the 'gagging of the Governor and Lady Murray is by written agreement'.

Cain conceded that there was an 'understanding' between himself, the secretary of the Department of Premier and Cabinet, George Brouwer, and the Murrays that there would be no further public comment. Cain tabled in Parliament a letter in which Sir Brian and his wife agreed to make no public comment on the circumstances surrounding the resignation. According to an *Age* editorial, 'The Premier, Mr Cain, who has long portrayed himself as the Mr Clean of politics, is looking a little soiled these days'.

The editorial stated that the Opposition was fully justified in giving Cain 'political hell' over the contrast to his approach in the 'much more serious matter' of Nunawading how-to-vote cards. 'The man who removed a Governor over an issue of propriety has left himself wide open to charges of selective moral indignation by his failure to demand stern disciplinary action against officials of his own party directly involved in a thoroughly grubby electoral tactic ... Victorian politics may be getting more interesting, but they are not getting any cleaner.'

The Prime Minister had yet to say what he knew about the 'big story' he had hinted prior knowledge of during his Queensland visit. Like many scandals in Victoria, the mystery surrounding Sir Brian's resignation faded out of the spotlight within months, with a 'gagged' Sir Brian and Lady Murray retiring to a vineyard near Canberra.

More than two years later, after a long battle in the courts, the *Herald* obtained documents under the Freedom of Information Act that cast new light on the intrigue. In evidence before an Administrative Appeals Tribunal hearing into the Herald's FOI application, Leonard Flanagan, QC, having headed the Continental investigation team, said he was 'inclined to believe' it was the Premier who had indicated in a conversation that he had heard a rumour that the Governor might have flown 'courtesy of Continental'. 'I was asked to ascertain whether that was so or not,' he said.

Documents secured by the *Herald* disclosed that police in the investigation team felt they had been ordered to 'deceitfully obtain' copies of the Governor's airline tickets and that they believed he had done nothing illegal.

14
The NSCA Disaster

Victoria's present Chief Commissioner of Police, Kel Glare, was first introduced to Australia's most mysterious man in 1979, when the Victorian division of the National Safety Council of Australia 'worked out of a tin shed at Morwell' in the lush farming region of Gippsland. Of course, Glare was not to know that the man known as John Friedrich would, 10 years later, cause the fire sale of arguably the world's finest private search and rescue outfit after totalling potential debts of up to $295 million. He would also spark one of the biggest alerts that Australia had ever seen.

Glare was impressed by the tenacity and coolness of the hard-working man with the soft German accent. 'He was a human dynamo, very demanding, progressive and a complete autocrat,' Glare said of Friedrich. It would have come as little surprise to the Chief Commissioner when, in January 1989 – by which time Friedrich had worked his way up the ranks to become the chief executive of the Victorian division of the NSCA – Friedrich was awarded the Order of Australia for community service, particularly search and rescue, in the Australia Day honours list. Glare was, after all, one of several people who nominated Friedrich.

Two years later – after a liquidator's hearing into the NSCA collapse, and a Federal parliamentary inquiry into the national security implications of Friedrich's quasi-military operation – the irony of his Order of Australia and his friendship with Glare is becoming apparent. The NSCA started in 1927. It was an incorporated body, which relied on subscriptions and user-pays principles for non-profit funding. Its clients included the RAAF, the Civil Aviation Authority and the Country Fire Authority.

Significantly, it was to be revealed in March 1991 that Glare's predecessor, Mick Miller, had actually set the ball rolling by initially nominating Friedrich for the Order of Australia. When Chief Commissioner, Miller had written to a director of the NSCA, James Guthrie, seeking his support for the nomination.

Like many people caught up in Friedrich's world, Glare had also been given warning signs that all was not right at the National Safety Council of Australia, Victorian division, which by then had its major operations base at Sale, Gippsland. On 21 October 1988, the chairman of the NSCA, Max Eise, had a brief meeting with Glare. Among other things, Eise told the Chief Commissioner that he feared that Friedrich may have been a security threat. Eise said checks on Friedrich's curriculum vitae showed he had falsified details, such as his place and date of birth, his education and his previous employment. Eise had been unable to find Friedrich's birth certificate and alleged former employers, and the school where Friedrich said he had been educated claimed he had never attended and that they had never heard of him. Eise had discovered that the town in South Australia where Friedrich said he was born was an abandoned mining town. According to the South Australian Mines Department, there had been mines there in the 1800s, but the area had been desert country for the past 40 years.

In February 1991, in a Supreme Court action over the NSCA losses, Eise told of having again contacted police following a phone conversation with Friedrich. When Eise had pressed Friedrich for details on a proposed business deal, he was allegedly told: 'If I fall off a cliff you'll go down with me.'

Eise had allegedly replied: 'I will be at the top waving to you as you go down.' Eise said Friedrich was 'an aggressive bugger' who was difficult to work with. The Supreme Court was also told Eise believed Friedrich could be an illegal immigrant. Eise was one of nine NSCA directors being sued by the Commonwealth Bank for $97 million that the NSCA, under Friedrich, borrowed from the State Bank of Victoria.

In an interview, Glare explained his reaction when Eise had gone to see him about the man he was about to nominate for the Order of Australia. 'I told him to check his records and come back to see me if there was any evidence. He did not come back,' Glare said. It was to be embarrassing when, less than two months after Friedrich did get his Australia Day honour, the *Age* on 22 March 1989, carried an announcement by the NSCA's acting chief executive, Colin Gomm, that the Victorian division was bankrupt and would have to wind down its air and sea rescue operations. That same day the Supreme Court was told by Ray Finkelstein, QC, for the NSCA, that there was a deficiency in the council's accounts of about $150 million. He said that about $50 million of the council's alleged assets could not be found, and that fictitious amounts of at least $50 million were listed in the accounts as debts owed to the council. He said there was a debt to the council's banks of about $103 million, most of which was unsecured and could not be met. No mention was made of Friedrich until the next day, when Finkelstein said the chief executive had resigned several days earlier and was the only person who knew exactly what had happened to the money. '... But we have had trouble getting information from him,' said Finkelstein. In hindsight, Finkelstein's understatement was almost laughable.

The Corporate Affairs Commissioner, Ron Trevethan, said the Supreme Court had made an order stopping Friedrich from leaving the country. His home in Heyfield, East

Gippsland, was empty and his car was missing. On 31 March, it was revealed that Friedrich used a credit card in Canberra, two days after his disappearance, to get cash from an automatic teller machine. A printout of his credit transactions showed his account had been debited from Cairns to Cooma, Gippsland and Melbourne, and that he had paid for supermarket goods, hire cars, restaurants, motels and souvenirs.

In the media, Friedrich was portrayed as a mysterious, ghost-like figure. It was evident that the newspapers were finding out as much about Friedrich as those whose job it was to find him. WHO IS JOHN FRIEDRICH? asked the *Age* on 25 March. This was the question faced by everybody seeking him and wanting him to explain the NSCA's finances. Speculation about Friedrich's background, his possible whereabouts and the possible intelligence roles of his operations at Sale coincided with the search.

Since 1985, Friedrich had travelled to America and Canada, without an Australian passport. One officer with an Australian security organisation had been unable to match his name to the flight manifest, after he boarded one international flight. It was revealed that Friedrich's marriage certificate and curriculum vitae gave conflicting details about his birthplace and age. Asked in October 1988 for his curriculum vitae, Friedrich had supplied a handwritten document. It said he was born on 7 September 1945, at Mt Davies about 30 kilometres from the junction of the borders of South Australia, Western Australia and the Northern Territory. However, according to his NSW driver's licence, he was born a year later, on 7 September 1946. There was further discrepancy still when Friedrich's marriage certificate was located. It said he was born four years later, on 7 September 1950, in Munich, West Germany.

Suspicions about Friedrich's background were further aroused when a journalist, who had worked on a local paper in East Gippsland, said he had been harassed by NSCA staff after publishing a series of articles about the organisation in 1986. Stephen Lamble, formerly of the *East Gippsland News*, said he had been followed, abused on the telephone, and at one time surrounded by NSCA staff in uniform. His articles had raised questions about some of the NSC's contracts and how the operations were financed.

News of Friedrich's disappearance quickly travelled overseas. A week after he was last seen, a newspaper in Munich reported that Friedrich was not who he purported to be. The newspaper said that he was one Friedrich Hohenberger – a man thought to have died in a skiing accident in Switzerland.

On 3 April, an editorial in the *Age* said there 'must be a searching public inquiry into the clandestine activities' of the National Safety Council. 'Nothing less than a royal commission, empowered jointly by the Federal and Victorian Governments, will suffice. Last week, we suggested that the two governments consider a public inquiry. Since then, more questions have been raised, and of a different and more worrying order, about this bizarre organisation and its secretive leader.' Speculation did not stop, and neither did the Australia-wide search, as Friedrich set out on a cat-and-mouse chase across the country. It was clear, however, that this 'secretive leader' was being none too cautious in covering his tracks.

At midday on 5 April 1989, Australia's most sought-after man stood on the side of a country road, in Baldavis, 50 kilometres south of Perth. He was waiting for a taxi he had just booked. About half an hour later a car stopped alongside him, but it was not the taxi he had been expecting – inside the unmarked police car were three detectives assigned to find him. They were led by a Western Australia detective, Glen Feeney, who got out of the car and had a brief chat with Friedrich. Feeney shook hands with Friedrich, who wore sunglasses, a red baseball cap, jeans, a red windcheater and casual shoes. 'Hi fellas, how are you?' he asked the other detectives in the car. He carried about $10,000 cash, but had no passport.

His 16-day flight had stretched from Gippsland, to Melbourne, to Albury–Wodonga, across the Nullarbor Plain by car to Kalbarri and Geraldton, 400 kilometres north of Perth. The day before his discovery, police did look out for him in Geraldton, but he had already returned to Perth by bus. From there he went to Baldavis and checked into Lakeside Caravan Park. He registered as Ian Paul. He told the owner of the caravan park, Helen Hawken, that he was on holiday and had arrived by bus from Sydney. During his stay at the caravan park, another camper became suspicious and reported Friedrich to police when he saw him loitering near a group of parked cars. By then police were too late arriving at the caravan park. Friedrich later returned and spent his last night of freedom alone in his on-site caravan. The next morning he took a taxi to a nearby hotel, where he paid the $20 fare and walked away. The taxi driver, Tony Harris, was suspicious so he circled the block. About 15 minutes later Friedrich hailed the same taxi, and they drove back to the caravan park. A few minutes later, Harris called his Fremantle base, which alerted the police. Meanwhile, Friedrich again called a taxi, but he got an unmarked police car instead. A Western Australia detective was quoted as saying: 'He is one of the friendliest guys I've ever dealt with … He's a very peaceful person, I'd say, and very likeable.'

Five days beforehand, he had felt far from peaceful. He was 500 kilometres north of Baldavis at the Anchorage Caravan Park when he wrote a long letter to his wife Shirley and their three children. The letter bore the name of Ian Hoskens, one of many aliases he used while criss-crossing Australia. Instead of reaching his home in Seaton, near Sale, it wound up in the hands of others. The note asked his family for forgiveness, and indicated he was desperate and talked of being at the end of the road and of ending his world.

Friedrich returned to Victoria, where officialdom and his own NSCA colleagues embarked on the long process of unravelling the financial mess. It became evident that there had long been warnings and that the NSCA debacle need never have occurred. On 13 May 1985, Dr Bill Suhr, of Peninsula Air Services, wrote to the then Premier, John Cain, warning that the NSCA was competing unfairly against smaller aviation operations. Almost prophetically, Dr Suhr warned that 'you cannot fly at cost and purchase millions of dollars of equipment at the same time', after saying that the NSCA appeared not to make a profit for some of its services. Cain later said the NSCA letter had not been referred to him. Dr Suhr died in a plane accident at Essendon Airport in 1986. A Liberal MLA, Graeme Weideman, then raised Dr Suhr's complaints with the Minister for Health, David White, who asked him to provide more information.

In early 1986, the chief executive of Skywest Aviation, Bill Meeke, wrote to the federal Minister for Defence, Kim Beazley. He claimed the NSCA was becoming a paramilitary operation and receiving covert funding from intelligence agencies or the Defence Department. Meeke said checks had been run on Friedrich's background, which showed that he had not taken a degree from a Queensland University, or worked for a New Zealand company, both of which he had claimed. Beazley later said no defence or intelligence agency had given money to the NSCA and that checks with ASIO found there was 'no reason to believe there was any untoward activity'.

Three months after the collapse, the public gained some insight into the elaborate rescue unit Friedrich had built when the liquidators, Price Waterhouse, advertised for sale the NSCA's equipment. Eleven aircraft (some of them military models), a 17-metre self-righting rescue craft, and Mercedes Benz tankers, prime-movers, horse floats and 'troop carriers' were all up for grabs. A Japanese consortium paid $530,000 for the NSCA's equestrian centre – reputed to be among the best in Australia. It was of little help. The next day Price Waterhouse announced that the NSCA's debt to creditors had reached $276 million – $65 million more than previously thought.

On 6 February 1990, shots were fired at Friedrich from a .45 calibre pistol, while he stood at the door of his home near Sale. Telephone wires to his house had been cut, and police said the gunman was standing at the front gate of the property. Friedrich used a portable phone to call police. On the one occasion that Friedrich talked to the media, he told the *Sunday Age* of having been courted by at least 27 organisations, including the celebrity agent, Harry M. Miller, for the rights to his life story. Miller described Friedrich as 'the catch of the century'.

15
WorkCare Blow-out

In mid-1989, the Victorian Government-run workers' compensation scheme, WorkCare, looked like being the State's biggest economic disaster. Only four years old, it had accumulated potential losses of around $4 billion: by 1992 this was expected to spiral to $9 billion. But between September 1989 and March 1990, WorkCare, like a chronically ill patient, underwent radical surgery and struggled back on to its feet; a full recovery even looked likely. It had been a long and painful illness – and its recovery was costly and divisive.

From its controversial beginnings and through its first four years of existence, WorkCare was plagued with problems, most notably its inability to withstand massive frauds and rorts that milked tens of millions of dollars from the scheme. It also failed to solve many of the problems it had set out to tackle. By mid-1989 it was the biggest lemon created by the State Government, one that threatened to bankrupt the State. But by early 1991 it was starting to recover.

When the ALP came to power in 1982, the desire to change the workers' compensation system was high on its agenda and promoted as one of the key planks of the new Government's economic reforms. It commissioned an extensive inquiry into workers' compensation and in 1985 announced its planned changes. The new scheme worked simply: instead of employers taking out insurance with private companies to cover them in case a worker was injured and then sued the company, everyone would be covered by a Government-run scheme. Every employer would contribute, with their risks assessed and premiums set at different levels. The top levels, however, were much lower than those paid in some high-risk industries. For a sawmill, for example, which faced a high risk of a worker being injured, it now paid a maximum of 3.8 per cent of its payroll – previously, its insurance company may have demanded 30 per cent.

Workers would no longer sue for compensation, a process that often took years to wind through the courts. Instead they would be paid at least 80 per cent of their wages while off work, and would be covered for medical expenses. An editorial in the *Age* agreed with the intention of the reforms, saying the old scheme was 'appallingly inefficient and unjust', and 'its costs horrendous, in both economic and human terms'.

'The scheme Cain inherited from the Liberals was a dilapidated, spluttering wreck,' the *Age* said. (Cain later described the old system, under which injured workers were given a lump sum for their injuries, as a disaster. 'Some bought a milk bar with it. I remember it well. Some paid their houses off, some had overseas trips, some pissed it up against the wall and went back on social services'.) Cutting out the old system hurt many who had made their living from it, especially insurance companies and lawyers.

The insurance industry launched a $2 million advertising campaign against WorkCare. The television and newspaper adverts were blunt: 'Was your train cancelled without warning this morning? It seems to happen a lot these days ... fact is, the Government department responsible simply can't get its act together. Again. Yet this same Government wants to take over workers' compensation. Hard to believe, isn't it?'

The legal profession also chipped in, with the Law Institute of Victoria sponsoring advertisements featuring a picture of a one-armed man. The caption said: 'What could be worse than losing your right arm? Losing you rights as well.'

Trade unions also expressed anger at the proposals and threatened industrial action. Along with employer groups, the unions were concerned about the lack of consultation, as well as the changes themselves, which were touted by Premier John Cain as 'the most significant social reform in 40 years'. While concerns were thrashed out (about the cost of the scheme, the rights of workers to take legal action, the rights to privacy and the level of benefits), the legislation was delayed.

One claim about the new system was ignored by the Government. David Slee, an actuary with Australia's then-largest workers' compensation insurer, C. E. Heath, said the numbers just didn't add up and the mathematics of the scheme 'were pure fantasy land'. He predicted, accurately, that within a few years WorkCare would fall into debt, costing more than the premiums provided. He said this would take six to seven years: it actually took half that time. However, the Government pressed ahead with WorkCare, taking out advertisements to promote the reforms that featured a picture of the Minister for Employment and Industrial Affairs, Steve Crabb, saying: 'We aren't going to get a better safety record by accident.' It gagged debate on the reforms in the lower house and pushed it through the upper house while the Government had a temporary majority, which it lost months later, after a successful legal challenge by the Liberal Party against a 'tied' vote in Nunawading Province prompted a by-election. And so, at 4 pm on 31 August 1985, WorkCare became law.

For some employers, the immediate benefits were enormous: in jobs that were traditionally high-risk areas for workers, premiums were effectively slashed. The metal trades industry estimated it would save $100 million in the first year. Premiums also fell in most sectors of the manufacturing, construction and timber industries. In some low-risk industries, premiums rose: it was cross-subsidisation, with low-risk industries effectively supporting high-risk ones. Overall, however, the Government proudly stated that average payments had fallen from more than four per cent under the old system, to about 2.3 per cent under WorkCare. It hoped the savings in the manufacturing and construction industries would encourage company growth and, in turn, boost employment by 25,000 jobs. However, many employers doubted this. They believed the low premiums would only last so long. They were right.

When WorkCare's first report was presented to Parliament, it said the scheme had a $25 million shortfall after only 10 months. The report warned that WorkCare might not be able to meet long-term financial targets if revenues stayed low, implying there was a need to increase employer contributions. Several months later, the Accident Compensation Commission – the body running WorkCare – said contributions for employers with bad safety records would rise.

By mid-1987 allegations of large-scale fraud began appearing, prompting Ken Crompton, of the Australian Chamber of Manufactures, to say: 'The way things are going it won't be long before employers will have more people on WorkCare than they have working.' Treasurer Rob Jolly acknowledged there were problems and that these were under review, but there was nothing serious. The review, he said, involved only 'fine-tuning'. He claimed that the level of fraud had dropped since the WorkCare system had been introduced. This seemed at odds with anecdotal evidence and the Government decision, only a few weeks later, to hire fraud investigators for WorkCare.

Four months later the Government revealed WorkCare's liabilities had blown out to $1700 million. These liabilities were the amount the Government faced paying to people who had already been injured. As there was no limit on the length of time for which workers could receive their weekly compensation payments, the Government had to make provisions to pay for as long as they remained off work – whether it be six months or 40 years. And worse, the number of long-term sick was steadily growing, thus the amount the scheme would be paying out grew. While WorkCare was taking about $700 million a year from employers, and paying out slightly less in its day-to-day operations, as more and more people joined the queue of the permanently out-of-work, WorkCare faced paying out more and more. And it would soon be more than it received each year from employers.

The Government moved to cut this number of long-term recipients by tightening eligibility conditions, encouraging people who had recovered to return to work, increasing the grounds for suspending or ending benefits, and boosting fraud investigations. Treasurer Jolly also announced that the employer levy would rise from 2.2 per cent of payroll to 2.4 per cent of payroll.

Jolly collated so many changes in his 'fine tuning' that there were 697 amendments to an Act of 276 sections. But these changes had only minimal effect on benefits and levies. Weeks later it was revealed the scheme's liabilities had reached $2680 million by June 1987 – less than two years into the WorkCare's life.

At this time, there were three main problems with WorkCare. First and foremost was that the numbers did not add up. The Government had underestimated the number of claims the scheme would attract, the cost of those payments and therefore the amount needed from employer contributions. Far more people were becoming 'injured' than under the previous scheme, despite a State Government program of worker education as well as emphasis on safety in the workplace.

Only just enough money was being taken from employers to meet the payments needed. But this did not account for the long-term injured, who would need payments until – or if – they got better. These were the unfunded liabilities, the ever-growing list of people who would have to be paid in the future. And the fact the list was growing was the second problem. There was little incentive to go back to work. People on sick leave were getting 80 per cent of their salaries (often supplemented to full pay), which developed a big number of rorts – people who 'became' sick and stayed that way. People became sick and found no good reason to go back to work, especially if they were on full pay. Employers found that women became 'injured' during their pregnancy. Instead of taking 12 months unpaid maternity leave, they could remain 'sick' and receive at least 80 per cent of their salary for as long as they needed. Only one doctor's certificate was needed to prove illness (each paid for by the scheme) and it was possible to shop around for the right certificate if the first doctor didn't give a 'good' enough prognosis.

On top of this were multiple rorts: people who claimed several benefits at the same time in different names, and those who claimed benefits from one job while holding down another. Investigations revealed that some ethnic communities became specialists in rorting WorkCare. Complete families would be on the scheme, all taking home at least 80 per cent of their weekly salaries while having nothing medically wrong with them. Unscrupulous doctors provided certificates and 'rehabilitation', in some cases referring people to clinics where meaningless tests were carried out at huge expense – all billed to WorkCare.

Age journalist Peter Stephens noted that the scheme had 'become a playground for doctors, physiotherapists and chiropractors'.

What made things worse was that if the Accident Compensation Commission suspected a rort and challenged someone's claim, it also had to foot the legal bill for their defence. The Accident Compensation Commission's legal bills skyrocketed. There was little to discourage people from rorting the system. Lawyers began advertising 'accident centres' and, with links to medical and rehabilitation centres, customers were passed through a system in which each player took a slice of the WorkCare pie.

Organised criminals became involved, taking a rake from the Government-provided scheme by either providing the unnecessary or overpriced medical and ancillary services, or recruiting drug addicts to become employed, instantly injured, then pass through lawyers, doctors and medical clinics while passing on a cut of their 'earnings'. The structure of the system was poor. From its inception, the Government sought to inform workers of their rights. Posters were put up in work places, claim forms were readily available. The culture developed that 'if you didn't take advantage of it you were a mug'. On top of the Accident Compensation Commission's limited powers in challenging claims, it found there was little room to investigate suspect claims. The original proposal, in deference to civil liberties, had banned surveillance, thus restricting the chance of proving that people were faking injury or ill-health.

Improved safety in the workplace – one of the scheme's key aims – was also failing. For employers there was little or no incentive to spend money improving safety and in some cases it deteriorated. In some areas of the public service, notably the police and education departments, large numbers of people went off on WorkCare. Many of these cases were later attributed to poor management decisions. The employees were not wanted, or performed poorly so, unable to make a decision about what to do with them – and instead of choosing an expensive retrenchment deal – they were encouraged to go on WorkCare. The money did not come out of the department's budget so it did not suffer – WorkCare just picked up the tab.

It was argued that some of the long-term sick on WorkCare, which numbered almost 20,000 at its height, were effectively unemployed, but did not appear on the State's unemployment figures. Instead of collecting the dole, they collected WorkCare, and artificially held down the State's official unemployment level. WorkCare was proving to be a nightmare. Many of the problems would be put right – they had to for the scheme to survive. Rob Jolly's raft of reforms of 1987 slowed some of the rorts, but overall they failed to stop WorkCare from becoming sicker and sicker.

When WorkCare was set up, Jolly pledged that over its first five years the average contributions of employers would be no more than 2.4 per cent. Days before the State election in October 1988, Jolly said he was confident this level would be met. 'I totally reject the Liberal Party claim that there should be an increase in premiums,' he said. But over following months it became clear that for WorkCare to survive, employer payments had to rise. The rorts also needed to be cut out, payments reduced and the number of long-term sick reduced.

Only weeks after the State election, a parliamentary committee headed by Labor MP Barry Rowe produced a 600-page report calling for numerous changes to WorkCare. Then, in May 1989, the Auditor-General, who looks at all areas of the State's finances, said WorkCare was facing a disaster and, to the embarrassment of the Government, said employer levies needed to be doubled to five per cent for the scheme to survive, making a mockery of Treasurer Jolly's confidence only months before. The State Government had four choices: lift premiums, cut payments, a combination of the two, or abandon WorkCare altogether. It chose the middle ground of higher premiums and lower payments, thus angering the union movement – which opposed any cuts in worker benefits – and the employers, who had to pay more to support the scheme. The threat of lower compensation brought protesting workers on to Melbourne's streets, disruption to public transport, electricity services and, ultimately, what amounted to a general strike.

It was a turbulent time. Premier Cain cancelled a trip to Europe because of the disruptions. The changes were condemned by the Victorian Trades Hall Council as callous and inhumane. The ALP's State administrative committee said the changes were 'clearly contrary to party policy and therefore totally unacceptable'. The ALP State president, Graham Bird, said the architects of the scheme were incompetent, accused some Labor MPs of weakness, and said the proposed changes were regressive. At the ALP State Conference, Premier Cain was booed and heckled as he made a speech defending the changes. The conference voted to reject the changes, but Cain said this would not stop his Government going ahead with them.

The opposition peaked with a State-wide stoppage on Wednesday 26 July, organised by the the Victorian Trades Hall Council under the theme: WORKCARE CUTS ADD INSULT TO INJURY. About 400,000 unionists went on strike for one day, the biggest show of industrial action in Victoria for 13 years. The Government, however, maintained it would not bow to pressure. The threat of a second, day-long general strike was abandoned when several key unions said they would not participate. The *Age* economics correspondent, Ken Davidson, said an increasing number of rank-and-file unionists were realising that the Government had no choice. He wrote: 'The union movement should not be in the business of disrupting the economy by protecting the interests of those who are rorting the system; interests that include doctors and lawyers as well as workers.' In early August 1989, Treasurer Jolly released a new set of reforms for WorkCare and the Trades Hall Council backed down on its threats of further industrial action. In effect, the Government had bitten the bullet and taken the hard decisions on WorkCare. Some of the changes broke – and others watered down – the promises of its original goals. Employer levies rose in broad terms from 2.4 per cent to 3.3 per cent and broke Jolly's promise of staying below 2.4 per cent over five years. Employers were angered by the increase, saying many businesses would move interstate because of the extra cost. The range of contributions was extended, however, making the system fairer; in other words employers paid more for their own risk and those with good records stopped subsiding those with bad records. Although the top rate became 7.7 per cent, new penalties meant employers with a bad safety record could be forced to pay a maximum of 23.1 per cent.

The 80 per cent of salary benefit was cut to 60 per cent for those people who had been on WorkCare for 12 months, although there were supplements for low-income families. The appeals system was tightened and the administration at WorkCare – which had become a byword for inefficiency – was purged. The patient, so to speak, is still on the road to recovery. In the 1988-89 financial year, WorkCare had unfunded liabilities of $4.2 billion and they were expected to top $5 billion a year later. In fact these, and other figures in mid-1989, forced Jolly to act. But after its dramatic surgery, WorkCare reported that in the 1989-90 financial year its unfunded liabilities had fallen to $2.5 billion. It expects to be paying for itself by 1995. The original financial ideals of WorkCare have not been met and, since the changes, workers have got less while employers have paid more.

16

The VEDC Affair

It was a vision. A vision of a brave new world where a Labor State Government would embrace and nurture private enterprise in a 10-year strategy to engineer economic security for a grateful populace. It ended in disaster, a shambles of such proportions that the reputation of Victoria as a sensible, conservative and solvent money centre went down the tube and with it the careers of some of Victoria's senior politicians. It started with a set of initials that meant nothing to most taxpayers – VEDC, the Victorian Economic Development Corporation. It acted as a merchant bank of sorts, an organisation set up in 1981 by a Liberal Government and revamped in 1984 by the Cain Labor Government. Its purpose was to lend money in the tourism and high technology areas – to promote business, jobs and prosperity for Victoria. The Cain administration saw it as a shining example of a Labor Government working together with private enterprise.

In 1984, the VEDC had $50 million worth of loans out. Within three years, that had ballooned to $259 million. The Government, outwardly projecting an image of frugal management, allowed the VEDC to run wild, loaning money without either ministerial or board approval. Corners were cut, regulations broken and the Act rewritten to allow borrowing at an unprecedented rate. Nine out of 10 applications for loans were accepted. Some would have been laughable if they had not been so tragic. Even as money was pouring out to just about anyone who wanted it, both the

Cain Government and VEDC were being promoted as astute money managers.

In 1987, the Government released 400,000 copies of a brochure bragging about the great gains in the State's economy. Entitled 'How Victoria has worked its way to the top of Australia', it certainly spared no adjectives in painting a glossy picture of the future. The brochure, which cost $125,000 of taxpayers' money to print, was lavish in its description of the corporation. 'The VEDC is backing Victorian industry with encouragement and money. Through the Victorian Economic Development Corporation, the Victorian Government is helping local firms strengthen themselves, particularly for the purpose of exporting.' The reality was that the VEDC was building up huge debts that it would never be able to recover. Put simply, it went from a relatively orthodox lending institution to one that carried far too many speculative, high-risk investments. It decided to gamble, and too often for a financial institution, it backed losers – big losers. Not only did the VEDC back them, but also it would top up loans in cases where it should have cut and run.

Fast and loose financial activities were not unusual in Australia in the mid-1980s, but the stock market crash of October 1987 shook out the people and groups that were overcommitted. But the VEDC seemed not to see the writing on the wall and kept lending as if the boom had not been lowered. From early 1988, it started to become obvious to insiders that the VEDC was in trouble. The Opposition raised matters that indicated real problems for the Government. In April 1988 the Opposition claimed that the VEDC was playing the stock market and losing. In August it began to attack the minister-in-charge, Deputy Premier and Industry Minister, Robert Fordham, over his involvement in a VEDC $12.5 million share float investment in troubled pharmaceutical company, Wallace International Ltd. The company later declared a $17.5 million loss. After the Opposition began to call it a scandal, on 29 August, Cain suddenly announced that there would be an election on 1 October, five months early. This meant that Parliament was closed immediately, effectively scuttling any attack under parliamentary privilege. The election announcement was so unexpected that it meant that the State Budget could not be passed until after the election. The timing also appeared to be strange, as it meant the four-week campaign would be conducted during the football grand final week and over two weeks of school holidays. The Opposition Leader of the day, Jeff Kennett, said the election was called so the Government would not have to answer questions in Parliament on certain scandals, including the VEDC. Cain breezily replied, 'There is always rubbish floating around in politics'.

The main finance writer at the *Herald*, Terry McCrann, wrote on 31 August: 'It's the hurried, desperately hurried, nature of it (the election) that suggests Mr Cain has something – plenty? – to hide ... This can only mean that he wants to get the election behind him before the dam bursts on the Victorian Economic Development Corporation and his Deputy Premier Robert Fordham.' On 1 September, Federal Liberal backbencher Dr Michael Wooldridge dropped a bombshell on the VEDC in the federal House of Representatives. He disclosed that a gold mining company, Whipstick Gold Mining Company Pty, Ltd, had been granted a large loan when its secretary had a 30-year criminal record and a conviction for manufacturing amphetamines.

A Victorian Government spokesperson confirmed a $450,000 loan to the company, saying: 'Before providing finance for Whipstick Gold Mining Company Pty Ltd, the VEDC carefully scrutinised the company's proposal, its financing and business plans. All the standard and appropriate financial reference checks were made on the applicant's credit history.' During the election campaign, the VEDC matter kept bubbling away, but tended to be lost or ignored amid various political claims and counter-claims.

On 1 October, the Cain administration scraped back into power for a record third straight term; then the wheels began to fall off. There was no honeymoon for the re-elected Government. Within weeks, the *Herald* revealed that Whipstick had a paid-up capital of $12 and tangible assets of only $27,000. Investigative journalist Ben Hills found that the ore crushing plant in the Bendigo area was operating illegally. Hills found that the two principals of the company, Alan Frederick Neilsen and his son, Alan, had long criminal records. According to the *Herald*, Whipstick applied to the Health Department for permission to use cyanide in a gold extraction operation. The department's chief drugs and poisons officer, Keith Moyle, had urged that the application be rejected because Neilsen senior had a prior conviction for producing amphetamines and that cyanide could be used in the production of the drug. After the newspaper revelations, the Government went into damage control mode. Cain said there was nothing new in the newspaper reports and did his best to hose down the issue, but it was just too big to go away. It was largely the now-defunct *Herald* newspaper that kept chipping away, refusing to be put off. Revelation after revelation about the VEDC battered the Cain Government, like a small ship caught in a cyclone. The Opposition, quite rightly, would not let go either.

The *Herald* found that more than 40 companies had collapsed after they were loaned millions of dollars by the VEDC. By November 1988, Cain announced that an inquiry into the VEDC would be conducted by respected accountant Fergus Ryan. If Government ministers thought the accountant's report would be the end of the issue, they were wrong. Parliament was recalled on 21 December so that the Ryan report could be tabled. It was a bombshell – Ryan found that the VEDC was insolvent with losses of $111 million.

Ryan also reported that it was chronically mismanaged and had been out of control. He found a lack of supervision, inadequacies in management, failures to check details on loan applications, lack of proper management procedures and the tendency to throw good money after bad. The report stated that loans were given in cases where credit checks had not even been done. Ryan found that loans valued at $2.75 million were made without VEDC board approval and stated that $8.25 million in loans were made without approval of Fordham, contrary to the Act. Information was found to have been withheld from people who were to make vital decisions within the VEDC. In conclusion, Ryan reported, the VEDC was a disaster, which fell short of criminal neglect. Even Cain then had to admit that the VEDC had been 'monumentally mismanaged'. Three days after the report was released, Cain went on holidays and Fordham took over as Acting Premier.

A clever way for politicians to deal with bad news is to release it just before Christmas and let it disperse over the so-called 'silly season'. If that was the plan for the VEDC issue, it did not work. When Cain returned to work in January, he was asked at his first news conference what should happen with Fordham. 'I do not want Mr Fordham to resign. I am not going to let this kind of discussion destabilise the Government,' he said. A *Herald* poll showed that the Cain Government would have lost power if the voters had known the size of the VEDC scandal before the October snap election. Fordham denied that his neck was in the noose and that he might be forced to quit, but they were brave words only. On 31 January, he resigned as Deputy Premier and as a member of the front bench. He was replaced as deputy by prominent Socialist Left member Joan Kirner, who would later become

Premier in her own right. Further revelations surfaced: up to 15 politicians lobbied the VEDC for loans for other parties. During a Freedom of Information case in the Administrative Appeals Tribunal, it was revealed that the Government moved hundreds of sensitive documents to an area exempt from FOI laws after the Opposition attempted to gain access to them. In February 1989, documents released under FOI showed that the Government had been warned that the VEDC was in difficulties a few days before the October poll was called. The VEDC chairman, Max Currie, wrote to Fordham on 18 August to resign, 11 days before the election was called. '... There will come a time when your support for me as chairman of the VEDC will become embarrassing for you and your position as the responsible minister and I feel that time is very close now. The time has come, Robert, for you and I to face up to the inevitable, hence this letter to advise you that the last meeting I will chair for the VEDC will be the October board meeting or earlier if you see fit. By this time all the embarrassing situations surrounding Fantasy Farm, Australian Vintage Travel, Islamic Abattoirs, etc, have been put to bed. Until the date of my departure, as mentioned above, I will continue to confront the news media and deflect as much attention as possible away from yourself and the Government.'

In the letter, Currie identified three major loans that were to create problems for the VEDC: Islamic Abattoirs was loaned $7.5 million, part of which was later found offshore with a Malaysian princess. Fantasy Farm, a poultry operation, collapsed owing $11 million. Australian Vintage Travel, a group specialising in luxury trains and ferries, went into receivership in July 1988.

Two weeks before the election, Currie had moved to defer a matter before the board because he was concerned it would damage Fordham. On 28 September, Currie wrote to Fordham saying he would resign on 30 September, the day before the election. Fordham wrote back to confirm the resignation would take effect on 10 October. Cain said he did not know about the 18 August letter. 'The first I knew of Mr Currie's resignation offer was a few days before the election.' On 27 September, Cain described the VEDC issue as a 'red herring'.

Currie had no banking experience when he was appointed chairman of the board in 1982. He told the *Age* that Fordham's department had been aware since early 1988 of the VEDC's worsening financial position, but it was encouraged to keep on lending. On 24 October 1988, the Government announced the scrapping of the VEDC, placing it under the umbrella of the Victorian Investment Corporation.

It was the end of the Cain dream and the beginning of the end for the Premier.

17

Loss of State Bank

The 1980s will be remembered as the decade of greed. Money made money, entrepreneurs were king and company takeovers were commonplace. All appeared rosy in the business world – until the share market crash of November 1987. In one day's trading, on what became known as Black Tuesday, the Australian share market shed almost one-quarter of its value, then continued to fall steadily in the following months. Overnight, cracks appeared in the paper empires of businessmen who had borrowed heavily to buy shares. While this was fine when shares kept increasing in value, their debts became disasters when share prices were slashed.

Much of the money lent to the entrepreneurs came from merchant banks, and the crash left many facing serious trouble. One bank that collapsed almost immediately was Rothwells, run by the Western Australian businessman Laurie Connell. For Tricontinental, the Victorian Government-owned merchant bank, nothing was said to suggest that the crash had had any effect. Tricon, by then one of the biggest merchant banks in Australia, had huge loans committed to the likes of George Herscu, Christopher Skase, Alan Bond, Joe Gutnick and Abe Goldberg, all of whom were to become financially crippled. Even after Black Tuesday, Tricon kept lending money.

One effect of the crash was that investors fled the share market and put their money into property and, as a result, prices soared. Combined with a Federal Government policy of ensuring there was plenty of money in the economy – it feared the crash could spark a recession and this was seen as the best way to prevent one – and a policy of the Cain Government of encouraging the building of offices in and around Melbourne, money poured into the building industry.

In truth, Tricontinental had been badly damaged by the share market crash, but now poured millions into the property boom which, like the share market, was set to collapse. Combined with high interest rates, many borrowers just found it impossible to meet their repayments. And the assets against which they had borrowed were, in so many cases, worth far less than the money they owed. When the first public rumblings of problems at the bank surfaced in early 1989, no one had any idea of the size of the problem. Certainly no one expected it to become Australia's biggest public financial disaster, one that would cost Victorian taxpayers around $700 million and the loss of their much-loved State Bank, the fifth biggest in the country.

One remarkable aspect of the Tricon saga was the speed at which it unfolded. Signs of trouble surfaced in news reports in early 1989, with suggestions of irregularities and illegal activities. By mid-year, attention focused on the fact that it stood to lose money. Twelve months later, in August 1990, with its debts haemorrhaging uncontrollably and losses put at $2.7 billion, the State Bank Victoria group was split up and the prize asset – the bank itself – was sold to pay for Tricon's mistakes.

Remarkably, as part of the deal, Victoria got to keep Tricon and all its woes. The $2 billion gained from the sale of the State Bank did not even come close to covering Tricon's losses. Victoria's taxpayers were left holding the carcass of a merchant bank that, over the next few years, will probably act as Australia's biggest debt collector.

Under the weight of the scandal, the Labor administration

ordered a Royal Commission into Tricontinental in late 1990. Headed by a former Federal Court judge, Sir Edward Woodward, the commission faced the task of finding out just how the small merchant bank grew at such an extraordinary pace, following a lending policy that turned into a disaster; to find out who knew about the problems, and when; to establish whether anyone in the group broke the law; and to probe the efficiency of the directors, executives, auditors and politicians involved in the Tricon debacle. The commission's hearings and investigations, aided by a team of lawyers, accountants and ancillary staff, were expected to cost the State further $5 million or more.

Tricontinental was set up as a merchant bank in 1960. It was not until 1978, under the Hamer administration, that the State Government, through the State Bank, acquired a stake in Tricon after Tricon became involved in a joint venture with a merchant bank. The State Bank had an interest in the merchant bank, and when things went sour, the State Bank emerged with 25 per cent of Tricon as a result of a rescue package.

In late 1984, two years after the Cain administration assumed power, it appeared that a Japanese bank might buy Tricon, but, after examining the books, it decided against the deal. Tricon, it seems, was not in good shape at that stage, although it was thought that it still had things going for it. It was at a time when banking deregulation in Australia was about to occur and most domestic banks were moving to make big changes to their operations. In March 1985 the State Bank bought out Tricon at a cost of $45 million, which was trumpeted as a good deal; it gave the State Bank a small-sized merchant bank that possessed a Hong Kong banking licence, a good entry into the world of high-profit, high-risk corporate lending.

The deregulation of the banking market changed the face

of Australian banking. To some extent the State Bank turned from a sophisticated 'piggy bank', which had supplied hundreds of thousands of Victorians with their first mortgages, into a vehicle that would lend to the high-flyers of the 1980s. Tricon's general manager in charge of lending, Ian Johns, was promoted to run the bank. He had been at Tricon since 1980 when he won the *Bulletin* Young Executive of the Year Award. Now, at 32, he was in charge of his own bank – and he aimed to make it the biggest and best in Australia.

In the days before the share market crash, Johns began lending at a furious pace. In three years Tricon's loan portfolio grew from $800 million to more than $4 billion, or about $3 million in new loans each day. And while the amount in loans increased, so did Tricon's profits. Tricon also won a reputation of lending money for risky ventures. While to some extent this is the role of a merchant bank – it takes more risks than the commercial sections of an ordinary bank – Tricon earned the name as the last port of call if all other loan facilities were rejected. For most borrowers in the days before Black Tuesday, big debts were not a problem while assets were also worth a lot of money. When the assets crashed, so did the chances of repaying the money.

What appears to have worsened Tricon's exposure to the share market crash was not only the calibre of the people and companies it lent to, but also the fact that some of those companies had multiple exposures: in other words, money hadn't been lent once, but more loans had been put on top of the original loan with questionable value on additional security. Combined with this, there were allegations of crooked practices within Tricon, allegations that have since been aired before the Royal Commission.

The first public inklings of problems at the State Bank came after the collapse of the Victorian division of the National Safety Council of Australia. The division had grown into a huge search and rescue organisation with planes, helicopters and water craft. In early 1989, accountants preparing the division's annual accounts found fictitious accounts and untraceable assets, and applied to appoint a liquidator. The State Bank had just over $100 million in loans to the division and looked like getting none of its money back.

At the same time, the State Bank had just acquired the small Australian Bank and was trying to sell Tricon to the new bank, with the aim of then selling equity in the larger, combined merchant bank. The deal was scuttled, especially because of concern about Tricon's level of bad debts. Instead, Tricon was absorbed into the State Bank. By that time, Tricon had already written off $31 million in debt for the 1988-89 financial year. Despite the losses, the merchant bank still expected to make a modest profit. Indeed, questioning about the State Bank and Tricon brought defensive comments from Bill Moyle, the State Bank's chief executive. In the *Herald*, Moyle was quoted as saying that there was no further indication of significant problems in Tricon and stories circulating in financial circles of hundreds of millions in non-performing loans were 'absolutely untrue'. Said Moyle: 'You must have the right systems in place and the right people and we have done that ... Our growth has been very prudently managed.'

Within three weeks, Moyle acknowledged that problems had grown. Preliminary figures for the financial year showed that Tricon had lost $82 million and the figure might be as high as $100 million. The Victorian Treasurer, Rob Jolly, advised of the problems by Moyle, described the losses as a 'once-off aberration' and said that the bank would return to a profit in 1989-90. On 10 October 1989, the accounts for the preceding financial year were finally released – and they were a disaster. For the first time in its history the State Bank had made a loss – a huge $197 million. The National

Safety Council debacle had taken $100 million off the bank's expected profit, then Tricon's post-tax loss of $275 million pushed the bank's accounts into the red. Incredibly, Moyle repeated the line that this was a once-off loss, and that the bank would return to profit the next year.

Since Tricon's lending had stopped several months before that October announcement, in retrospect it was to seem curious that losses of only $275 million had been identified. Within a year, losses had ballooned to around $2700 million. It appeared that each time a new set of auditors studied the Tricontinental accounts, millions more in bad debts were found.

It was revealed that the Tricon side of the bank had outstanding debts of $300 million to two companies alone: Christopher Skase's Qintex and the then-staggering property company Interwest. A bank spokeswoman said provisions for these debts had been made in the annual accounts. Since these were only two companies, and there were many more with huge borrowings that faced collapse, speculation provoked a political outcry. The State Opposition began pushing for an inquiry. Treasurer Jolly said then there was no need for one as the State Bank had made provisions for all liabilities. Jolly's words returned to haunt him as more and more bad debts emerged.

In February 1990, an auditor's report prepared by Touche Ross revealed almost $800 million more in bad debts, taking the State Bank's total bad debt to almost $1.4 billion, of which around $1 billion was as a result of Tricon loans. The Government announced the replacement of five board members – including chairman Bill Moyle – and said it had banned the State Bank from any high-risk entrepreneurial lending. But even more debts began emerging. A Supreme Court injunction was taken out by the State Bank against the *Sunday Herald* to prevent the newspaper publishing a list of some companies owing money to Tricon. A list of debts was then leaked to the Victorian parliamentary press gallery, and found its way into newspapers and on to television and radio.

The ever-increasing losses and the general state of the Victorian economy were ideal ammunition for the Liberal and National Party Coalition as it fought a federal election on 24 March 1990. The Opposition lost, but made huge gains in Victoria. On 29 March, Rob Jolly, who had become increasingly isolated from the Socialist Left faction, resigned as Treasurer. He cited instability in the Labor Party and said: 'The pressure imposed on my family in recent times has been intolerable.' In the preceding weeks pressure had been building for him to resign over the State's economic woes and Tricon in particular.

Some weeks later, the international ratings agency Moody's downgraded the State Bank's credit rating. Then word began filtering out that the Government was considering selling the State Bank. The Government replied to the first report of the problem by saying, rather curiously, that the bank was not for sale, but that any offers would be considered.

On 7 August, as the prospect of a sale began to firm, Premier John Cain resigned. His decision was not so much inspired by the State of Victoria's economy and the pressures of the State Bank fiasco, but more the schismatic state of the Labor Party. Rumours about his leadership had surfaced regularly in the preceding five months and, as Cain said in his resignation statement, 'for a Government to be effective it needs to be united behind its leader'. He had lost that support.

Cain's successor, Joan Kirner, found that the State Bank was her most immediate worry; and the only solution when the mathematics were studied was to sell it. Its debts were now confirmed at around $2.7 billion, yet the bank itself was worth only $2 billion. To keep the bank would mean meeting interest payments on the $2.7 billion, something totally unaffordable for Victoria in the economic circumstances.

A deal was struck whereby the new Socialist Left Premier was to sell the publicly-owned bank to another publicly-owned bank, the Commonwealth, leaving the Federal Government in the position of having to sell 30 per cent of the Commonwealth Bank to pay for the acquisition. Kirner described Tricontinental as 'an unmitigated disaster' and the decision to sell the State Bank as 'difficult but necessary'.

The State Opposition threatened to block the sale of the bank, but changed its mind after a series of briefings, when it was reportedly told that if it blocked the sale, overseas investors might withdraw their money from the bank and it would collapse altogether. The banking fiasco was to mean more bad news for Victorians. With the State retaining Tricon and its debts, and receiving only $2 billion from the Commonwealth, the Government foreshadowed plans to also sell the State Insurance Office, the Government's share of the profitable Portland aluminium smelter and various pine plantations, to help pay off the outstanding $700 million. On top of that, a report by two Melbourne University economists predicted that the sale of the State Bank alone would mean 4000 job losses in Victoria.

Many found the situation hard to comprehend. As *Age* columnist Stephen Bartholomeusz observed: 'It is almost inconceivable that a financial institution could lose so much money so quickly.' In an editorial, the *Age* said the scale of the disaster seemed barely credible. The paper urged a thorough inquiry. 'Victorians are entitled to believe they have been grossly betrayed. They want to know how such a thing could happen.'

The State Bank's new chairman, Ralph Ward-Ambler, whom the *Age* described as 'luckless enough to become chairman of the doomed bank', said the Tricontinental losses were inexplicable. 'We are just overawed by what we have seen ... If you went out to search for people who had a very poor chance of staying in business it would have been hard to do better.'

18
Pyramid Collapse

At the start of 1990, rumours began circulating in the financial world that Victoria's largest building society, Pyramid, a wholly-owned subsidiary of the Farrow Corporation, was in deep trouble. Another widely circulating rumour was that the two directors of Farrow Corporation, Bill Farrow and a former Geelong football hero, David Clarke, wanted to sell Pyramid. Clarke went public, saying that Farrow Corporation – the name behind four major Victorian building societies; Pyramid, Geelong, Federation and Countrywide – was simply the victim of jealousy from other banks and building societies, who were less aggressive in the marketplace and couldn't offer depositors such attractive interest rates.

'At the moment, everyone has rumours about everyone ... If we take $100 million in deposits in any given month, where is it coming from? ... If we heard of another building society in trouble, we would help, but it makes you angry to track the rumours back to them,' Clarke said. There is no doubt that, at the time, Clarke's words were aimed at allaying the fears of the 200,000 Victorians who had an average of $10,000 in the hands of one of his building societies. Within days, on 13 February 1990, the Cain Government, too, moved to avert a run on Pyramid by assuring customers the society was in a sound financial position.

Still trying to battle through its third term of office in Victoria, with the hangover of several unprecedented financial catastrophes – including the VEDC, Tricontinental and

National Safety Council debacles – the Government's assurance would prove to be yet another multi-million dollar glitch, the cost of which would eventually be borne by every Victorian taxpayer. It would also put another nail in the coffin of Labor's flailing electoral hopes and of Premier John Cain's chances of retaining the leadership. It would finish as well the Cabinet career of the treasurer, Rob Jolly, who called a joint press conference with the Attorney-General, Andrew McCutcheon, after being approached by Clarke and Farrow about the affect of the rumours.

'We have checked the matter out: they have a strong liquid (assets) position, the back-up of a national banking system behind them and, consequently, people should feel very secure about the funds invested in the Pyramid Building Society,' the Treasurer said. The accompanying statement, released to the media, said: 'The Treasurer, Rob Jolly, and the Attorney-General, Andrew McCutcheon, said today depositors' fund in the Pyramid Building Society are secure. There is no reason for people to withdraw their funds. Withdrawals are totally unnecessary and only create difficulties for customers. Rumours circulating about the society are without foundation.'

Little more than two months later, on 24 June, the Government appointed an administrator to the Pyramid, Countrywide and Geelong building societies and all assets were frozen. Farrow Corporation had been put into the hands of an administrator, Ken Russell, of the accountancy firm Coopers and Lybrand, on the recommendation of the registrar of building societies, David La Franchi. Major aid agencies, such as the Red Cross, the Brotherhood of St Laurence and the Salvation Army were immediately asked to offer short-term help to depositors whose assets had been frozen.

However, while Cain was willing to assist the depositors in terms of human resources, he immediately ruled out any

Government assistance for the corporation or its depositors. 'I do not believe the suggestion that the taxpayers ... should underwrite the activities of organisations out there borrowing in the public sector is a tenable one and I don't intend to pursue it.'

On 26 June, Stephen Bartholomeusz, finance writer with the *Age*, commented that while the Government had no legal obligation to bail out Pyramid depositors, it had 'a considerable moral obligation' to do so. The same day, the *Age* editorialised: '... It is also embarrassing to the Government, especially in the light of the statement made by the then Treasurer, Mr Jolly, that depositors' funds were secure. To desperately worried depositors, that confident announcement of a few months ago contrasts uncomfortably with yesterday's stand-off remarks by the Premier, Mr Cain.' The editorial said: 'It could be argued that in making its February pronouncement the Government raised false expectations about just what it was prepared to do to support Pyramid and its parent group, Farrow Corporation, in the event of a collapse.'

Unknown to the depositors, the Government, the registrar of building societies, the directors of Farrow, and other banks, had for months been aware that the rumours circulating about the the building societies were, indeed, not without substance. In February 1990, at the same time that Bill Farrow and Cain's Cabinet were assuring Victorians that their deposits with Pyramid were safe, David La Franchi was secretly thrashing out a rescue plan to save the group. The deal would be simple: Pyramid and Farrow Corporation could keep taking deposits, but a lending moratorium would be imposed until a buyer could be found for the group. The brakes finally were being applied to Farrow and Clarke's high speed race down the high-risk, rapid-growth track that epitomised the group's prominence and success in the 1980s.

The key problem was, that while a buyer was desperately being sought, the Farrow group continued its high-profile advertising campaign and continued to accept millions of dollars from new depositors.

Also unknown to depositors – secure after their reassurances from Treasurer Jolly – Clarke and Farrow, old mates from Geelong College, were bankrolling high-risk commercial property developers. But the dreams of Farrow and Clarke crashed along with the commercial property market at the end of 1989. In the mid-1980s, trusts and myriad holding companies were developed for the Farrow Corporation. Regulations forbid the expansion of building societies outside their own State, so the trusts and holding companies became ideal hiding places for unwanted exposure to the property markets and to allow the company's rapid interstate and overseas expansion. Farrow operations could be opened in other States through separate companies. On the surface, the company's balance sheets appeared straightforward. Under the surface, they included dangerous exposure to the commercial property market. Such exposures only became known to other financial institutions when they were called upon, secretly, to rescue Farrow Corporation, and privately searched the company's loan portfolio.

Ironically, it was the 1987 stock market crash that amplified Farrow Corporation's ultimate difficulties. After the crash, investors were shy of the stock market and sought the safety and relatively high interest of bank and building society deposits. At the end of 1987, Bill Farrow gloated that his group was taking $5 million a day in deposits – Pyramid alone was taking $2 million, he said. In the two days before Christmas the group took more than $14 million, often from new depositors.

While other building societies grew rapidly in the year after the crash, at a rate of about eight per cent, Farrow Corporation grew by a massive 53 per cent. In the same period, its assets jumped from $400 million to $1.1 billion.

All money lenders make profit by paying interest on deposits and lending at a higher rate. But in mid-1989 the margin between Farrow Corporation's loan and deposit rates was becoming slimmer and the group was forced to rely for profitability on up-front loan fees. To keep its massive funds coming in, the company began offering even higher interest rates on shorter-term deposits. Clarke and Farrow could blame rumours for the eventual run on their building societies, but it was the high-risk nature of their deposit portfolio that made them so vulnerable. Pyramid was also especially vulnerable because the average depositor had $10,000 invested compared with the average $3000 investment in other Victorian societies, and up to 30 per cent of the Farrow group's deposits were raised through borrowing from the inter-bank market. Investors became increasingly concerned about lending to the group as word about its heavy borrowing spread.

By the end of 1989, Bill Farrow was meeting secretly with the Victorian Corporate Affairs Commission. His message was simple: he and Clarke wanted out. Informed sections of the finance media were pleaded with not to publish stories about the group, lest they cause a run on the societies' funds. They took Clarke's assurances that the group was safe and obliged. While the meetings continued, Farrow Corporation's lending margins were being further squeezed. In the previous six months, interest on loans was $230 million, compared with the $218 million interest paid on deposits.

In the four months before the group's assets were frozen, Bill Farrow and David La Franchi desperately sought a buyer. In February, Farrow was coolly reassuring his customers they were safe in his hands while he continually informed the Corporate Affairs Commission, the Cain Government and the Registrar of Building Societies about the woes of his group. After the group's assets were frozen, the Friends of Pyramid – a lobby group for Farrow group depositors – was born. On 29 June, up to 2000 depositors marched on Parliament House, pressuring the Government to bail them out. It was evident that Geelong, the home of the Farrow Corporation, was bleeding. Thousands of people, who had trusted their life's finances to the group, had no access to their money. There were reports of suicides as family nest-eggs were feared lost and social security recipients had no access to their money. The dreams of hundreds of young married couples saving for home deposits and lured by promises of high interest, were shattered. Graeme Wallace from the Friends of Pyramid said a woman had rung for him while he was not home. She wept while she explained to his daughter that she was on the verge of overdosing on sleeping pills.

As the pressure mounted, the ALP caucus realised that unless it offered financial aid to Pyramid depositors, any slim electoral chance it retained would be dashed. So, on 3 July, the ALP caucus forced Cain and his Cabinet to cover at least $1300 million in funds to unsecured depositors. This would give depositors between a 20 and 25 cent return on their deposits. Cain said: 'We are going to ensure that depositors, the people who put their money into Pyramid as ordinary depositors, are looked after. No matter how long it takes, that $1.3 billion is assured, is what I'm saying.'

The Secretary of the Trades Hall Council, John Halfpenny, was quick to say that the Government's back-down over financial assistance to depositors would not enhance Labor's chances at the next poll. He said there had been no attempt to emphasise the responsibility of Farrow and Clarke for the demise of Pyramid depositors.

On 13 November 1989, a Supreme Court judge – who was

hearing evidence as part of an inquiry into the Pyramid collapse – ordered Farrow Group administrator Ken Russell to stop shredding the company's documents. On the same day, the building societies were placed into liquidation after Farrow issued a notice of motion for winding up the company.

Although Pyramid depositors had in the order of $2500 million invested, the ultimate cost to the State Government and in turn Victorian taxpayers remained unknown. But one thing was certain. The financially embattled Victorian Government, by then led by Joan Kirner who had replaced John Cain, could not foot the bill for the Farrow Corporation out of available funds. A new petrol tax, introduced in haste by the Government, and to become known as the Pyramid Tax, would ensure that every Victorian motorist helped foot the bill for the Pyramid collapse every time they went to the bowser – for years to come.

19
Shadow over Opposition

Throughout the political crisis surrounding the downfall of Premier John Cain and continuing disquiet following his succession by Premier Joan Kirner, adding to the despair of Victorians was the perception that there was not an effective, acceptable State Opposition.

During most of the Labor Party's rein after it gained power in 1982, the Opposition Leader was Jeff Kennett, an irrepressible advertising whiz kid, who fought two elections, missing out on becoming Premier in the second election, in 1988, only by the narrowest of margins. By rights, he should have been Premier. His had been a virtual lone voice – that tended to be ignored by a gullible media – shouting warning and concern over the direction in which Victoria was heading.

A flamboyant, but sound politician, Kennett became the victim of Victoria's cultural left establishment, which used the media to deride rather than listen to him. In retrospect, he was embarrassingly correct.

Unlike other States, significant sections of Melbourne's media have long ignored any semblance of journalistic professionalism or balance in treatment of non-Labor politicians, regardless of issues. Kennett's treatment was recalled on 24 February 1991 in a special article by *Sunday Sun* State political reporter, David Wilson, formerly Kennett's press secretary.

Referring to members of the Victorian parliamentary press gallery as a 'mouse pack', a variation on the term 'rat pack' used to describe members of the federal parliamentary press gallery, Wilson wrote: 'It could be argued that the mouse pack's synchronised Kennett-baiting in the run-up to the 1988 election prevented a Liberal win – and paved the way for continuing multi-million dollar State Government losses.'

Just three days before Wilson's article, Neil Mitchell, commentator on radio 3AW and formerly editor of the *Herald*, acknowledged what had happened in an on-air discussion on whether the Cain Government was able to rush to the polls in 1988 and hoodwink Victorian voters before they got to know the full extent of its financial mismanagement.

'One thing I do remember very strongly,' said Mitchell, 'was the way Jeff Kennett was campaigning as Leader of the Opposition on things such as the VEDC. And he was right! He was shouting at people. He was shouting at the media: for heaven's sake, take notice, have a look at what's happening ... up until it was established [to be right], to the eternal discredit of the media. And I include myself in it. I did not look closely enough at the time. I thought I did. I didn't. We didn't listen. Jeff Kennett had tried explaining. He didn't have it all locked up, but he did have the sniff of it and he tried everything to get people to take it seriously and didn't get anywhere.'

At the very time Kennett was finally being seen to have been right, and thus perhaps right for the time, the Liberals themselves ditched him in May 1989 in favour of a lacklustre ex-country mayor, Alan Brown, with an unfortunate political past. In Parliament, after he succeeded Kennett, one Cain administration minister, Steve Crabb, labelled him the 'Arthur Daley of Wonthaggi' a derisive reference to the fictional character Arthur Daley in the popular *Minder* television series.

As mayor of Wonthaggi, a coal mining centre in Gippsland,

Brown became embroiled in a controversy that has never ended. A carpenter who became a builder and businessman, Brown was elected to Wonthaggi Council in 1970, becoming mayor in 1974. In 1977, while mayor, he signed a planning application form for the building of five flats at 218A Graham Street, Wonthaggi, on behalf of a company called Hagel Pty Ltd, of which he was a director.

The following year, a row erupted over permission being granted to Hagel Pty Ltd to build the flats in breach of planning regulations. Brown by then had been endorsed as Liberal candidate for the electorate of Western Port. Perhaps the victim of dirty tricks, Brown's electoral office was ransacked and files set alight in circumstances in which police concluded the fire had been deliberately lit.

Late in 1978, an *Age* 'Insight' story under the headline LIBERAL CANDIDATE FACES PROBE disclosed that two Government departments, Planning and Local Government, were investigating a complaint over the flats built by Hagel Pty Ltd. In May 1979, Brown was elected to Parliament. Three months later, the then Minister for Planning, Lou Lieberman, wrote to Wonthaggi Council advising that his review of a Crown solicitor's opinion in a report of a committee of inquiry 'leads me to the conclusion that your council's decision to prosecute is right'. In August 1980, Hagel Pty Ltd was fined $300 and ordered to pay $970 in costs in the local Magistrates' Court for breaching the Town Planning Act. Three months beforehand, Brown had resigned his directorship.

On entering Parliament in May 1979, Brown attracted publicity when he listed Hagel Pty Ltd among assets on the pecuniary interests register. It disappeared from his register for the following five years. When it was relisted in 1986, a Cain administration minister, Neil Pope, suggested Brown had been in contempt of Parliament for having failed to properly disclose his business interests.

An all-party parliamentary committee subsequently cleared him, concluding that he had declared his own interests within the law. Brown had explained to the committee that it was his wife, Paula, who had an interest as a beneficiary of a trust of which Hagel Pty Ltd was trustee. The committee accepted that Brown had not considered his wife's interest in the trust to pose a material conflict between his interests and his parliamentary duty.

As disclosed in the *Sunday Age* on 4 February 1990, in a special report by Brendan Donohoe and Tom Noble, a hitherto secret report by a departmental committee had found that Brown had breached his civic duty over the Wonthaggi flats issue. Donohoe and Noble obtained documents under Freedom of Information legislation. The documents related to a committee of inquiry set up by Brown's former parliamentary Liberal colleague, Alan Hunt, when Hunt was Minister for Planning. The committee's report stated that, as mayor at the time, it had been Brown's duty to ensure that there was no departure from council's planning policy.

'In particular,' the report stated, 'he was in breach of his civic duty in making application for a permit for five units which he knew, or should have known, was not in accordance with the council's planning policy and which, moreover, conferred upon him an advantage which was not available to other persons who had previously and have since been granted permits for the erection of four flats on sites of approximately a quarter of an acre.'

The report noted that the Graham Street site was generally overbuilt, was not in sympathy with local development, and that spaces at the rear and side of the flats were less than required by council permit. Consideration was given to applying to the Supreme Court to force Hagel Pty Ltd to alter or demolish the flats, but this was decided against on the grounds that it would have caused severe hardship to both the company and tenants of the flats.

Another file released to Donohoe and Noble documented a complaint by Wonthaggi council. In June 1981, the council had passed a motion calling on the Premier, the Minister for Local Government and the Leader of the Opposition to investigate actions of Brown in 'standover tactics against council re 218A Graham Street flats issue'. The complaint had arisen over a telephone conversation between Brown and Wonthaggi's town clerk, Tony Deed – 13 months after Brown had originally disassociated himself from Hagel Pty Ltd and just over a week before the hearing of an appeal by the company before the Town Planning Appeals Tribunal.

In July 1981, Deed wrote to Local Government Minister Lou Lieberman saying council had 'sharply reacted' to what it saw as 'stand over' to have it 'play dead' in the appeals hearing. His letter stated: 'It strongly resented this attempted interference in council's decision process ... If Mr Brown is no longer involved in Hagel Pty Ltd, why is he seeking to influence the council in resolving the outcome of the planning permit difficulty?'.

The documents contained a letter of response to Lieberman from Brown, in which he said he was acting as a responsible citizen in telling Deed that Hagel Pty Ltd had been advised to sue the council in the Supreme Court if the council won the case before the appeals tribunal.

It was disturbing, Brown wrote, that the council should have placed a 'distorted interpretation on his call. It is regrettable that the council should have chosen to interpret information offered in the spirit of goodwill in the manner that it has, and that it should have used such intemperate language in a letter to yourself [Lieberman], the Premier and the Leader of the Opposition, to express its feelings'.

A haunting aspect of the unforgotten Brown episode is that Brown was elected to Parliament to replace a Liberal backbencher, Doug Jennings, who was expelled from the party for speaking out publicly and crossing the floor in Parliament in condemnation of the Hamer Liberal Government during debate over land scandals that eventually crippled the Liberal Government and paved the way for the ascendancy of Labor's John Cain.

20

State of Despair

On 4 January 1991, Victoria witnessed a true people's revolt when thousands marched through the streets of Melbourne in what will go down in history as probably the State's largest public demonstration. It was a spontaneous outpouring of despair over the state of the State, inspired by a solitary man, Danny Johnson, a proverbial battler from the bush.

Johnson, a demolition contractor, thought up the idea after a groundswell developed in response to a letter he wrote to his local newspaper at Warracknabeal in which he deplored the economic and political plight of Victoria. As a popular 'uprising', it was a graphic demonstration of people's power. Although embarrassed officialdom sought to play down the size of the crowd, estimates ranged from 50,000 to 150,000.

The doyen of newspaper columnists, Keith Dunstan, writing afterwards in the *Sunday Age*, recorded: 'In 40 years I have been in many marches through the city, including two protesting against the war in Vietnam, but this was bigger and in many ways more impressive than any of them.' Terry Vine, writing in the *Herald-Sun*, observed: 'It proves that a man can still get a hearing in this great land of ours, no matter where he is or what his station in life.'

Apolitical, Danny Johnson, speaking from the back of a truck outside Parliament House, said: 'My concerns are with politicians of all parties. The Opposition at the moment provides no real alternative to our pathetic Government that has sent the State down the tube. In fact, the leadership of both sides of politics needs a real shake-out. We, the silent majority, must become the vocal majority. We have taken the first and most difficult step in making our State of Victoria great once again. Today, we have welded a bond between city and country Victorians that will never be broken ... We're regaining something lost. The Anzac spirit is reviving.' The rally demanded a fresh election, without delay. His wife, Sheena, was to remark afterwards: 'He stands where Lech Walesa stood a decade ago at the dawn of Solidarity.'

In an open letter to the Premier, Joan Kirner, the editor of the *Sunday Sun*, Ian Moore, took the Premier and her political colleagues to task for seeking to dismiss the massive rally as a 'nuisance'. 'Much to the shame of your people,' Moore wrote, 'there were attempts to link the rally with extremists of the Right, an idea eagerly promoted by some sections of the media.'

The *Age* in particular attracted criticism. In a response published by the *Age* itself, Peter Boyle, national director of the Australian Small Business Association, criticised *Age* writers for disparaging and lampooning Danny Johnson. 'Danny Johnson has become the target of attack because he was successful. If he had drawn a crowd of, say, 1000 people, then the *Age* could have comfortably ignored him. But confronted – perhaps affronted is a better word – by the awesome reality that, in the space of three weeks, an unknown battler from the bush could inspire perhaps 100,000 people to march the streets of Melbourne, your writers conclude that this level of popular involvement is dangerous and that there must be a conspiracy involved. What balderdash. Only people living in an intellectual ivory tower could reach those conclusions. The march was, in truth, a cry from the heartland of middle Australia.

'Would the *Age* have condemned as dangerously manipulated the crowds in East Berlin, in Riga, in Bucharest, in Prague, in Warsaw, that tore the heart out of the communist governments? Danny Johnson did not deserve to be lampooned by the *Age* for his energy and courage in initiating the Save Australia rally. It was an eloquent act of quiet desperation by a man who is passionately worried about his children's future and the future of the nation. If the *Age* finds something to deride in this, then it is sadly out of touch with the feelings of Victorians and with its own historical roots.'

More than 100,000 signatures were subsequently collected for a petition to the Governor of Victoria, Dr Davis McCaughey, calling for an election. On the day of the protest, it was announced that the number of people in Victoria receiving unemployment benefits had risen by 50 per cent to well over 100,000 in the previous six months, ahead of the national average. About 600 people a day were joining the dole queues. Bankruptcies in 12 months had risen by 70 per cent, compared with 32 per cent for the nation as a whole. While days lost through industrial strife dropped nationally by more than 32 per cent, Victoria's actually increased by nearly nine per cent. Exports from Victoria dropped by 30 per cent, while there was an increase of 7.5 per cent for the rest of Australia.

As the State's credit rating was downgraded on the international monetary stage, with a State Budget blown out to a deficit of almost $800 million, shops and factories closed and farmers were forced off their land. Victorian property values plunged by $2.5 billion and car sales slumped by 40 per cent. The number of companies placed in receivership almost doubled, with Victoria representing more than 36 per cent of all business failures in Australia. The manufacturing sector was decimated. Businesses began fleeing the State, mostly heading to New South Wales. Welfare agencies were flooded with calls for relief.

It might have been a recession in metropolitan Melbourne, but even the State's agriculture minister, Barry Rowe, acknowledged that it was a depression for rural Victoria. Not for 100 years had Victoria faced such a plight. It was reminiscent of the great recession of the 1890s, when Victoria was worse off than elsewhere in Australia, more so than during the Great Depression of the 1930s, when few farmers were forced off the land.

As Geoffrey Blainey observed in *Our Side of the Country*: 'Its effect [the 1890s recession] was less the loss of money, but the loss of confidence ... official enquiries into why institutions had become bankrupt revealed enough evidence of corruption to erode confidence even further. Too many directors and managers of financial institutions had been quietly robbing the till or cooking the balance sheets.'

At a State Government level, the recession of the 1990s focused on gross political mismanagement.

Under the State Budget, Victorians were slugged $12 a week more, with the auditor-general, Ches Baragwanath, disclosing that State debts totalled $32.6 billion.

Aside from the demise of the Victorian Economic Development Corporation and sell-off of the Victorian State Bank, Victoria faced the sale of its State Insurance Office, Gas and Fuel Corporation, State Electricity Commission power generating plants, a 35 per cent stake in the Portland aluminium smelter as well as State pine plantations and a host of other assets.

Avenues for the Government to borrow more were limited. As it was, the Government already faced deferred payment of up to $750 million in repayments to investors who had put money into the Victorian Equity Trust, set up in 1987 to raise money outside limits set by the Loan Council. The money was, in turn, lent to the Board of Works, State Electricity Commission and Gas and Fuel Corporation. People encouraged to invest in the trust were offered a 'put option' under which the Government pledged to buy back their units by mid-1992.

In a State 'fire sale' of a multitude of assets, Crown land used as parks was sold for building blocks, and day nursery buildings were sold for restaurants. In all, 300 pieces of Crown land were snatched for quick sale. Also 28 court houses, nine schools, public pools, halls, fire stations, hospitals and even jails. All were deemed 'surplus to requirements'.

A total $3.6 billion in State assets were earmarked for sale.

Unannounced, the Government began selling off the entire rolling stock of Victoria's public transport – some 1500 trams, trains and buses were sold to foreign banks and finance companies. Under a $1.2 billion leaseback arrangement, repayments were deferred until 1997 and 1999 when a future administration would have to worry about it.

In earlier deals, the Government had incurred stock market losses of $918 million as well as foreign exchange losses of $714 million. Unfunded superannuation liabilities were estimated by the auditor-general's office to have reached $16 billion.

The auditor-general intervened to disallow one amount of $35 million in spending, personally approved by Treasurer Tom Roper, involving a complex interest-rate swap entered into with an overseas merchant bank. The money, received up-front, was used to discharge a debt obligation of the State Bank of Victoria, later sold to the Commonwealth Bank. To offset the amount, the Government had to reduce funding from budget programs. Otherwise, under audit regulations, Roper and officials could have faced personal liability for the money.

The chief director of audit, Russell Walker, said: 'We regard this matter with the utmost concern as it goes against fundamental principles of parliaments that operate within the Westminster system.'

The auditor-general criticised the Government over the introduction of 'scratch' tickets for public transport users. The system, known as MetTicket, caused a month-long strike, leaving trams blocking Melbourne streets. The ill-fated scheme was found to have been based on a survey of only 100 people. Once abandoned, it was discovered that 25.9 million tickets had been pre-printed, enough in some cases to last 137 years.

The auditor-general also criticised the Government for allowing the run down of $1.1 billion of Government buildings, necessitating $46 million to make them meet building, fire and safety standards. It was stated that the buildings were under used, cost twice as much to operate as privately-owned offices, and were hamstrung by a deal between the Trades Hall Council and the Ministry of Housing and Construction that meant repairs were carried out at an 'excessive cost'.

Auditor-general Baragwanath was praised in a *Herald-Sun* editorial for 'continuing to pursue his courageous and invaluable role as official whistle blower'. The independence of the auditor-general is enshrined in constitutional statute.

Not so fortunate was the chairman of the Urban Land Authority, John Lawson, who was removed from his position after resisting what he saw as a possible illegal transfer of funds. The Government wanted him to use money from a $12 million infrastructure fund, drawn from the authority's reserves, to spend on projects across the State that were outside the authority's normal charter. The authority is the main supplier of urban land for housing, with concessions for first-home buyers. In four years under Lawson, accumulated profits in cash and assets had doubled to $128 million, with the Government receiving $40 million.

Similarly, Victoria's official keeper of public records, Chris

Hurley, was stripped of his office and statutory powers after he wrote a 'please explain' to the chairman of the Public Service Board, Maurice Keppel, about the shredding of documents.

The Ombudsman's office tackled the Government over the handling of public transport funds, after it discovered that employees were being paid to do nothing, at a cost of $500,000 a month, because the Government had given a commitment not to sack anyone. The public transport budget had overrun by $40 million by the end of 1990, mainly on wages and salaries.

There was further embarrassment when the Premier of neighbouring NSW, Nick Greiner, lashed out at Victoria, blaming rising unemployment in Victoria on the Government for running 'sheltered workshops' for public servants. Victoria's public service had risen by 30,000, at four times the rate of increase for the rest of Australia.

A report in January 1991, prepared for the Federal Government by the Institute of Public Affairs, damned Victoria as the most inefficient State administration, saying it could save up to $2.4 billion a year just by cleaning up its act and reining in spending. With its public service overstaffed, it managed to give inferior service than in other States.

Since the election of the Cain Labor Government in 1982, important sections of the public service had been stacked with political appointees. By the time John Cain resigned in August 1990, his popularity had dropped to 18 per cent. Cain was regarded as middle-of-the-road Labor, though hamstrung by Socialist Left power brokers who were instrumental in ousting him in favour of their favourite, Joan Kirner.

Kirner became the first Socialist Left and the first woman Premier in Victoria. Though she pledged to govern for all, she was to come under continual fire for doing the bidding of the socialist left who had given her the job. She came under particular criticism soon after becoming Premier when she visited a union picket line in a much-publicised dispute at the Hoechst chemical plant. She was seen as close to John Halfpenny, a former communist who had joined the ALP and became secretary of the all-powerful Trades Hall Council. Halfpenny became such an embarrassment that she later sought to distance herself from him in the public mind.

Among other things, Halfpenny outraged the public by seeking to sabotage a deal by 300 workers at the Shepparton Preserving Company, who were prepared to accept pay cuts to save their company – and their own jobs. Halfpenny warned: 'The company won't succeed or survive if they try it.' A modified deal was eventually approved.

On Christmas Eve 1990, when countless workers but no union officials had lost their jobs, it was disclosed by the *Herald-Sun* that about half of the 58 staff working under Halfpenny at the Trades Hall Council were being subsidised by taxpayers through State Government grants totalling nearly $1 million a year – almost equal to what the THC collected in affiliation fees from its 132 unions. This prompted the *Herald-Sun* to comment editorially: 'Racked by debt, it [the Government] nevertheless finds in its depleted money vault a whopping $1 million a year for the Trades Hall Council, a body dominated by the politically-active forces of the Socialist Left whose soul mates also dominate Spring Street ... Trades Hall chiefs remain a protected species.'

Joan Kirner also suffered politically by being linked with Wally Curran, secretary of the Meat Industry Employees' Union, and a leader of the Socialist Left, who had been her political mentor. For more than a year, Victoria's meat export trade had been disrupted by Curran-led union disruption, costing more than $100 million in meat exports. In less than 10 years, the number of Victorian export abattoirs fell by half. At the same time, other States increased their meat exports. Victoria previously had been Australia's leading beef exporter, but by 1991 was exporting less than $300 million out of a national total of well over $2 billion.

Ian Mackay wrote in the *Herald-Sun* that farmers believed Premier Kirner and agriculture minister Barry Rowe were 'unable or unwilling to take on Mr Curran because of his powerful position with the ALP Socialist Left, and that this is an abrogation of their responsibilities towards the State'.

The *Herald-Sun*, a merger of the morning *Sun* and afternoon *Herald*, became strident in its denunciation of strikes and union power. In a volatile political situation, it emerged as a new force in its own right in Victorian public life. With a massive daily circulation of well over 600,000, largely inherited from the *Sun*, it introduced daily editorials, whereas the placid *Sun* usually refrained from any comment at all. In its editorials, the *Herald-Sun* pointed to what it saw as union lunacy, even commenting, 'Visitors, after all, are already asking themselves about the mental state of Victorians'.

It was a theme taken up by Shaun Carney in the *Age* at the end of 1990. He quoted a Sydneysider: 'Yeah. They're mad down there' and a Brisbane man saying, 'They're up themselves'. Carney lamented: 'Melbourne people, Victorians generally, lost something this year. They lost their self-respect. In some ways they lost Melbourne; it is not the Melbourne most of us knew ... Until recently we considered our city to be Sydney's rival for Australia's premier metropolis. In the face of our despair about ourselves, Sydney's arrogance about itself, and the facts, it is hard to see how we could really make that boast now. This year may mark the time in our history when we – the people of Victoria and the State Government – finally ditched that self-delusion.'

It was a truism that underlined the aura of despair as a once-resilient State faced a long haul of revision and recovery.

Index

BBP Book Offer

PO Box 337, Seaford, Victoria 3198

Please send me the following books (indicate number of copies in the boxes):

☐ *Shadow of Shame* (Bob Bottom)

☐ *Bugged* (Bob Bottom)

☐ *The Godfather in Australia* (Bob Bottom)

☐ *Untold Violence* (Tom Noble)

Please send my books to:

Name____

Address______________________________________

________________________ Postcode_______________

I enclose $__________

being $14.95 per copy (includes post and packing)

☐ Cheque ☐ Money order